Adorning the Bride

Reflecting the Stones of the Breastplate

By Angela Noe

ISBN: 979-8-218-03102-2 (Angela Noe)

Picture on Cover by Claudia Addison

ACKNOWLEDGMENTS

I cannot begin to thank the many persons that have blessed me in so many ways to accomplish writing *Adorning the Bride*. From the moment this book started, it is Yahuah that deserves so much gratitude. I honestly am still in awe at how this came to be. I felt like He placed jewels in my hand and let them sparkle, illuminating His Word, His presence, and then shining those sparkling gems across a canvas of deep friendships.

From when Sue Ellen Barton called me and asked me about having a woman's retreat in my home to the many I meet even now, to whom I know will be blessed by the sparkles of these gems, Yahuah has had His hand in this. Those that attended the retreat and those that joined the first time I shared this Adorning the Bride have been such a positive influence in my life and in writing this book. I want to mention the many encouraging me to write and thresh out this book. Thank you, Airey, Alesha, Amy, Amanda, Annette, Darlene, Dawn, Heather, Jo-Anne, Rebekah, Rita, Susan, Suzanne, Suzy, Teresa, Tracy, and Vicki. It could have only been the Master Jewelers' hand. He not only encouraged me, but He bound us together through some deep discussions and some losses. Amid the study, we lost our dear friend Suzanne Messersmith, but the Messiah let us see how He can sparkle through even the difficult times.

Oh, how I thank each of you for your encouragement and love and thank Yahuah for showing us how He loves through our friendships. Speaking of beautiful sparkling friendships, Bonnie (Tekoa) Manning has blessed me with not only the constant words of calling me an author but also pushing me to give birth to this study. She even helped me find editors and helped to get *Adorning the Bride* published. Bonnie not only poured out love to me, encouraging me to write, but she took my inability to write a blurb and put her beautiful authorship into place. Thank you, friend. Also, to Bonnie's husband, Jeff, who took all the technical burdens of publishing off of my shoulders, I give thanks. To my editor, Jo Zausch, who made me feel confident in my ability to write and also became a heartfelt friend, thank you.

Yahuah kept placing special friends into my life. To my sweet friend Julie Gibertini who took her time in reading through the words, carefully discerning and advising me on what one could perceive and helping me look for errors not only in writing but also in my heart, I cherish you. Yahuah even designed a plan for my neighbor, Claudia Addison, to paint a masterpiece for the cover; again, thank you. I feel that my list of acknowledgments is genuinely endless. There is not a week that goes by that someone else steps into my life that I know Yahuah wants to share some of these treasures. I want to thank each of you for being such a tremendous blessing in my life. Thank you, Yahuah, for molding a setting for sparkling jewels that show us many ways to shine.

All my love,

Angela Noe

Table of Contents

Introduction

A. OPENING

Please read. This is not just an introduction.

Before reading this book, please understand that it comes from a walk as I sought for God. As Scripture states, there is a cost when we are seeking Yahuah (God) with all our heart, soul, mind and strength. You will find that I use the name Yahuah for God. I chose 2 translations for Scripture reference that use either Yahweh or Elohim. I use Yahuah and those Scriptures because of a personal testimony and feel they best proclaim His name. I refer to Jesus as Yahshua to clarify who He is. There are some Hebrew terms that you might not be aware of; I pray that doesn't distract you. Instead, I pray that it intrigues you to learn more. I have provided a glossary with some of those words in the back. I found that as I study His Word, His language, His culture – Him-- that there is a never-ending deep water that becomes more and more refreshing with every sip. There is a thirst for more. The irony is that the more refreshed I get the more difficult it is to continue through the trials that will come. But at the same time, the more refreshed I get with learning about Him the easier it is to ignore the difficulties. I ask you to take time to read the Bible verses. His Word is the sword that will penetrate your thoughts, heart, and even your soul. I so desire that He will speak to you and make this book have meaning to you. In fact, that is my prayer for you as you read this. Also please take time in answering the questions. Don't think of this book as something to hurry through to finish reading. Instead, I pray that this book will fill you with deep waters that reflect through you like beautiful stones across your soul. Hence the title. . .

Adorning the Bride

"-Reflecting the Stones of the Breastplate-"

B. UNDERSTANDING

Why This Book

In February of 2019 I was able to have a women's retreat in my home. This book was originally written with women in mind, but as the book developed, I realized it was for everyone. The retreat was rather remarkable because the place I live is about one and a half hours away from most of the persons who attended, and I either did not know them or had just recently met them. I desired to have a retreat in my home for many years and was astonished that Yahuah (God) was opening the doors for that to occur. As I was preparing for this retreat, I kept feeling that Yahuah was telling me to go to the weekly Parasha (Torah reading) for that week and to connect that reading to the role of a woman. I planned to discuss the role of a woman from Hebrew definitions of words such as woman, wife, female, helper, and mother but felt as if I needed more direction. So, I began reading through the Parasha reading of that week which was T'tsaveh, Exodus 27:20-30:10.

This reading starts off with commanding the sons to bring pure oil to keep the light burning. As I prepared for the retreat, I concluded that we first need to listen to Yahuah; in order to listen we must have pure oil so He can shine through us. Our role, male or female, can quickly fall apart if we are not listening to Yahuah.

Because I was preparing for a woman's retreat, I was still looking for definitions for female. Part of the definition of a female is that we are a pit, like a setting created to hold a beautiful jewel. Like a mother carrying a baby in her womb, we are created to be fruitful. I don't only mean fruitful as in bearing children but in bearing the fruit of the Spirit also. Even though this is part of the definition of the woman, both men and women are to be fruitful. Both are created to be filled with the Spirit and become shining jewels. We truly need to have pure oil, truly need to listen for His voice with a deep understanding that allows us to shine with purity.

Because the role of believing in God has become so muddied and impure and because the role of men and women is distorted, it is so important to learn to hear His voice. Example: the role of a woman can quickly shift from being treated as no more than a piece of property to being a demanding feminist. The role of the man can shift from being a tyrannical overseer to a passive and insecure child. I came to the conclusion that I needed some direction in knowing what to write, how to hear His voice. As I continued to read the Parasha –T'tsaveh, I came to the stones that are on the breastplate. The breastplate, known in Hebrew as the Choshen Mishpat, is part of the garments of the High Priest. It was when I began reading about the stones that I knew why I got that nudge to connect this week's reading to the roles of a woman; and actually to the role of any believer –male or female, young or old. I felt that Yahuah opened the doors wide and began showing me things about each one of the stones. We have garments to wear, wedding garments. Since we are to be priests, 1 Peter 2:9, I realized that part of our garments could be like the breastplate. Not that we are the high priest - only Yahshua (Jesus) is the High Priest, but we are to be a reflection of Him.

The jewels are to be set in pure gold; they are beautiful, they sparkle, and they are transparent. I realize that there is confusion on the stones, in fact, not even the name of each stone remains consistent in different translations; however, I feel like each one can represent a character that helps us to be transparent before Yahuah and allows us to shine like beautiful jewels. Would you like to shine brilliantly before Yahuah (the one and only God), reflecting the character of Yahshua? Can you be His translucent special treasure? Can you put on the garment that reflects who He is?

Dear Abba, the Master of everything, pour out Your heart. I pray that You, Yahshua, will shine brightly to every corner of my soul, to every corner of the heart of anyone reading this book. Please show us how to reflect who You are. Show us how to join ourselves to You. Show us Your heart Yahuah. Amein.

C. LONGING

During some trials of what seemed like must be the final days of my life, I was so alone. Everyone had turned away from me as if every word I said would cause them disgust. I so longed to receive truth from Yahuah that all I could do was think about getting more. Like a newborn baby longing for pure milk, I wanted to understand more about Yahuah's Word. I didn't want to be deceived, I didn't want to say one thing and do another, I had no desire to slander anyone, no desire to be right, nor was I envious of others; I just wanted to know Yahuah. I wanted to grow closer to Him. I so desired to be a living stone, brightly shining, precious in His sight. I was so rejected by man but felt I was becoming part of His spiritual house. I wanted to be set apart for Him. There were many things I sacrificed in order to be closer to Yahuah. Many did not understand my desire to learn more and they pushed away from me. Although I longed and still long to be closer to them and to share the things Yahuah has and is showing me, an awkward space developed between us. How I longed to be able to share with so many I love, the things I was learning but every time I shared; the farther it would push them away.

All my zeal was on my Savior;
a precious cornerstone.

Then, the deeper I believed in Him, the more I was not disappointed. This precious cornerstone began to shine brightly in my heart, more valuable than anything this world could ever offer. Though I am still stumbling through disobedience to His Word, I am learning every day how to love and obey and I have a longing for pure milk that satisfies beyond explanation. Crossing over the threshold into the presence of my Savior brought emotions of unworthiness but He lifted my head and explained that I am part of a Royal Priesthood, chosen for His own possession. He gave me a calling to proclaim how excellent He is. He pulled me out of this deep darkness and brought me into His light. He began to dress me in the beauty of garments that reflect His. Beautiful transparency reflected on each of the stones of His garment as He showed me to wear these every day in everything I do. To keep these as a reminder of how I need to abstain from fleshy lusts which wage against the soul. Keep your behavior excellent among everyone, so that in the thing in which they slander you as evildoers, they may because of your good deeds, as they observe them, glorify Yahuah.

I felt like Yahuah handed me each of these stones, precious and sacred. He showed me something about each one of them as He dressed me to reflect Him.

Chapter 1

חושן משפט Choshen Mishpat (the breastplate)

Before we go into detail about the stones, let's briefly mention what the breastplate is. It is called **חושן משפט** *Choshen Mishpat*. *Choshen Mishpat* represents priestly judgment. This is thought to be symbolic of the high priest's garments for 2 reasons:

1. If the priest errors in his judgment there is atonement for his mistakes.

2. It gives the divine connection to give godly judgment.

As we know Yahshua is the High Priest, so obviously there will be no error, and He is of complete Godly judgement. Therefore, as He is our High Priest, it is important to take note of the fact that the *Choshen Mishpat* covers the heart. I think of this covering as when Yahshua returns as judge, He will hold the tribes close to His heart as He judges. This thought again supports my thought on the character of these stones. Just as we do as parents, when our children are walking in a way that has pleasing character, we hold them closer to our hearts. We always love them, but truth is they are closer when they walk in a pleasing way. Same goes with our relationship with Yahuah. When we walk out His commandments --walking in a pleasing way-- we get in a closer relationship with Him.

John 14:15 If you love Me, keep My commandments.

It is a place of beauty and transparency where we *da'at* know Him. The breastplate is worn with the *ephod,* which is similar to an apron that covers the front and back.

Chapter 2

אפד *Ephod (the apron)*

The apron that the high priest wears is the *Ephod*. The Hebrew letters for the word *Ephod* are א *alef*, פ *pey*, and ד *dalet*. (We will refer to the meanings of Hebrew letters frequently. For more about the meanings of the Hebrew letters please see the chart on appendix A). The letter *alef* represents Yahuah the leader, the letter *pey* represents the mouth, and the letter *dalet* represents the door. If we combine the meanings of these letters, we can conclude something similar to the following: Yahuah is speaking at the door. Remember the breastplate of judgment lays on the heart. This combination of the *Ephod* and the breastplate is a place of being judged by His heart at the door where He speaks tenderly desiring us to wear the wedding garments He offers.

So, as we look at each stone, I hope that we can begin to wear His garments. First, I simply took the letter meaning of each stone, and then I came back and looked for verbal roots in each word. Some of them are a word found in the Hebrew language, some of them I broke the words into smaller words. I found what the *Ruach HaKodesh* (Holy Spirit) showed me to be humbling and encouraging at the same time.

In scripture it states that the stones represent each tribe. I think there is much to understand about their representation. I am barely touching the surface of any significance of them. There are so many more attributes to learn. For now, I just want to see how to make it applicable. Maybe the connection to each tribe also represents a certain character that we need to wear. Maybe the naming of each stone also connects to the name of each tribe at each of the gates to the new temple. I know this for fact . . . if we are going to be dressed ready for the coming bridegroom, *Yahshua HaMashiach,* Yahshua the Messiah, we need to wear the garments He desires, the ornaments that shine transparently to reflect Him. Therefore, in the following discussion of the stones I decided to intentionally not focus on the stone as in ruby, jasper, amethyst, etc. I want the focus to be on a character not on the type of jewel. The list of stones are in order according to Exodus 28:17-20.

Chapter 3

אדם Odem Stone

I knew Yahuah was loving, everlasting, merciful . . . but how could I truly be redeemed. The adversary surrounded me on every side. I was wandering, running, crying, lost. I was so hungry so thirsty for something to satisfy my soul. I felt I could not hold on any longer. I cried loud with restless writhing. Like a storm out of control, I could not be satiated. In darkness like death, I was imprisoned in misery and in chains. I couldn't hear any counsel from Yahuah, I cried louder

"Please God, save me from this turmoil!" The waves were crashing all around me, pounding on the shore. The storm was rushing in like an uncontrollable force, every part of my being was about to be destroyed. But then He came and gently shattered the iron tethers that held me useless. I couldn't respond I only stood in awe – I could barely breathe – everything simply stood still. The waves that were crushing on the shore stood still, the pounding storm and howling winds were silenced; my soul was miraculously satisfied and all was quiet.

I breathed deeply as His springs of water filled my thirsty ground. He rebuked the winds and the sea and it became perfectly calm.

I was amazed; what kind of man is this that even the winds and the sea obey Him?

This is the understanding of the first stone placed on the breast plate… the one of being still, the one of being in awe of Him. This is the Odem stone, the precious stone of being in perfect stillness, perfect awe of our beautiful Savior.

If we take the definitions of the Hebrew letters in the word Odem **אדם** (again look at Appendix A for more understanding of the letters) we get **א** *alef* which represents the leader or Yahuah; **ד** *dalet* which represents a door or at the door; **מ** *mem* which represents water or being of water. If we separate the **א** -which represents Yahuah- from the rest of the word, then the rest of the letters leave the word for blood, **דם** *dom*.

א *Yahuah* -- **דם** *blood*

So, we can see this word as Yahuah connected to the blood. This word אדם is the word for *Adam* human, but this word is also the word for *red*. All of these words have something to do with productivity and stillness. But you may ask "How can something be productive and still at the same time?" An example would be that red is the first color a person can see. It is the first thing a baby will take notice of. It is what causes one to be still in order to take in the color. In other words, learning to be still so that one can produce or grow in understanding. It is the thought of being still so that we can be in awe of Yahuah. There are other words that include this root of the letters **דם** *dom*.

דמה *damah* means to be still as in when the sun stood still. It is the ability to be still. We produce and grow when we learn to be still. Note the letters **ד מ** in the following verses.

Psalm 131:2 Surely I have set myself and quieted (ודוממתי) my soul; like one weaned by its mother. My soul in me is like one weaned.

Psalm 4:4 Tremble do not sin, speak within your own heart on your bed and be still (ודמו).

This is a stillness, a quietness where Yahuah resides. It is the calmness of the sea in Matthew 8:23-27. (Please take time to read Matthew 8:23-27.) This character teaches us to be still, in all circumstances.

Many Hebrew words have a contranym (a word with opposite meanings), and many of our characters can also have a contranym. On the positive side it is the stillness in Yahuah when we are in awe of Him, when we stop and take notice of Him, when we listen to Him; on the negative side it is when we begin to think we are a god, that we can face our fears on our own, struggles, etc. without trusting Him. We think we are the stillness. We should not try to be the one in control nor the one that everyone has to do as we say. We see this negative use of the root word of the *Odem* stone- *dumah*-דמה in *Isaiah 14:14 …I will be compared (אדמה-adumah) to Elyone (the Most High).* Our stillness has to be connected to Him or we just turn back to worthless dust.

Odem, as stated, means being red. It is like the blood and is also connected to the wine that is squeezed out. Thinking Hebraically, if you have blood you should be producing. This requires one to be in awe of Yahuah and to be willing to be squeezed out in order to bring pure oil. To be an offering completely in awe of Yahuah.

Romans 12:1-2 Therefore, brethren, I call on you through the compassion of Elohim to present your bodies a living sacrifice, holy, pleasing to Elohim which is your reasonable service. And do not be conformed to this age, but be transformed by the renewing of your mind, in order to prove by you what is the good and pleasing and perfect will of Elohim.

The first stone is one of learning to be still, to be at peace, to trust Him completely. Wear this stone and be still, listen to His voice. Let the voice of Yahuah be like the sound of rushing waters that calms your soul.

Revelation 14:2 And I heard a sound (voice) out of Heaven, as a sound of many waters, and like a sound of great thunder. Also I heard a sound of harpers harping on their harps.

Chapter 4

Applying the Odem אדם Stone

1. Think of at least 2 things in your life that keep you from being able to be still.

2. Many things take away our ability to truly be still before Yahuah. Many things take away our ability to be able to look up and say 'Wow! The storm just stopped!' Go through the following list and apply something in your life to each situation.

A. When thinking of finances, what is your biggest struggle? Are you struggling to get bills paid, are you worried about retirement, are you stuck in a rut and can't get ahead, are finances your focus? Write out very specifically anything that takes away your stillness in relation to finances.

B. What is your relationship with your father like? Was he in your life and did he make you feel loved? Was he too much your buddy or too much your disciplinarian or was he simply not there? Was he focused on only himself and not you? Did you or do you appreciate all he did or does for you? What is at least one thing that comes to mind that takes away some of your stillness when thinking of your father?

C. What is your relationship with your mother like? Did she nourish you and listen to you or did she ignore you? Did she train you in the way to go or did she teach you to go with the flow? Was she focused on you, or was she distracted? Did you or do you appreciate her? Did she make you feel loved? Do you make her feel loved? What is at least one thing that comes to mind that takes away some of your stillness when thinking of your mother?

D. If you are married or in a relationship, what is the first thing that comes to mind that upsets you in that relationship? Does that relationship make you feel secure or does it cause you to feel afraid? Does that relationship lead you closer to knowing Yahuah or does it become the distraction that you focus on instead? Do you feel united or more alone?

E. What are your goals? List at least two. Do you lose stillness in Yahuah worrying about making that goal? Do you feel inadequate at achieving something? Does that goal become your focus instead of Yahuah? What do you feel Yahuah gifted you with in order to serve Him? Do you lose your ability to trust Him that He will bring that gift to fruition?

F. If you have children, what is your relationship with each of them? What aspects of being a parent cause you to lose your stillness? Do they show you love, do they obey, do they become your only focus? Do you show them love without any expectations? Are there hurts that have caused a distance between you and them? Most importantly are they following Yahuah? What is the biggest thing you desire with your children that would bring you peace, stillness?

G. Admit it or not, all of us have some type of fear. What fears do you have? Are you afraid of failing, afraid of some person in your life, afraid of getting sick, afraid of not having money, afraid of being immunized, afraid of not being immunized, afraid you will be like one of your parents, afraid of being alone, afraid of being wrong, afraid of being rejected, afraid of not knowing Yahuah? Write down at least 2 things that cause you fear.

In order to be still it is true that you must cast your burdens on Yahshua. He died for you to bring you peace. He died so that we can have hope and in that hope we can be still.

1st Peter 5:6-11 Then be humbled under the mighty hand of Yahweh, that He may exalt you in due time; "casting all your anxiety onto Him," because it matters to Him concerning you. Be sensible (sober spirit), watch, because your adversary, the devil, walks about as a roaring lion, seeking someone he may devour; therefore, resist him, being steadfast in the faith: and know that the same sufferings befall your brethren that are in the world. Now the Elohim of all grace, who has called us to His eternal glory by Yahshua the Messiah, whom Yahweh has given to us, will strengthen us to endure these little afflictions that we may remain steadfast and established in Him forever. To Him be the glory and the might forever and ever.

Psalm 46:10 Be still (cease striving) and know that I am Elohim! I will be exalted among the nations; I will be exalted in the earth.

Exodus 14:14 Yahweh will fight for you; and you be silent (still).

John 14:27 "I leave peace to you; My peace I give to you; not as the world gives, I give to you. Let not your heart be troubled, nor let it be timid."

Memorize at least one verse that relates to being still and letting His voice calm you. Apply that verse to the situation that causes you the most distraction from stillness in Him.

Chapter 5

פטדה Pit'dah Stone

You pulled me out of the turmoil, out of the storm by giving me Your comfort. You were able to calm me, even in the midst of trouble. I stood there tested by the raging storm and You stepped out in my place. I watched as the storm tossed you beyond your control, beaten, mistreated, betrayed, slandered… then you were lifeless;

You suffered in my place.

In Your agonizing pain You gave me comfort through Your love. You took my sins on Your shoulders. You truly died in my place. How could I ever thank you? What was I supposed to do now? Through Your gift of death, You rose and gave me life. A life I didn't deserve, an eternal gift that nothing can compare.

I sing praises to You, eternal Savior.

Oh, Yahshua how could you love me so dearly and comfort my soul. I praise You; I give thanks to You. You gaze upon me as if my sins are no more.

You look at me as if I am treasured, pure and clean. I beg for mercy and You grant me purity, I turn to You in repentance and You look deeply into my soul and wash away my humiliation with Your blood. Why, oh why my soul, do you still pour out like brackish water? I praise You with thanksgiving but then out of my mouth comes careless words. You placed a bridle over my mouth and guided me, separating words of condemnation and complaining from words of thanksgiving and praise. I sing praises to You; I will not be silent.

I give thanks to You forever.

Give thanks to Yahuah for He is good, His love endures forever.

This is the Pit'dah stone. It is a stone of thanksgiving and praise. A stone of guarding one's mouth, having no bitter root within you.

This stone might be a topaz, but again I don't want to focus on the color or type of stone. If I look at the letters of this word, the letter פ *peh* represents the mouth, the ט *tet* can refer to something of the serpent, the ד *dalet* is the door, and the ה *hey* means beholding, breath, or giving honor. So, we could say the mouth of the serpent is at the door beholding or giving honor. That sounds confusing – the serpent is beholding or giving honor? But the letter ט *tet* can reveal both good and evil. In fact, there is a teaching about the letter *tet.* If the letter *tet* is broken into two it would be made from the letter *zayin* ז and from the letter *vav* ו. And then the bottom of the letter *vav* would be bent. The bent *vav* symbolically represents being humbled. The letter *vav* representing a humble man bowing before the king. So this letter *tet* can represent a humble man bowing before a king, yet it also can represent a snake coiled around in a striking position. The letter *tet,* meaning serpent, can also mean a humbled man bowing. This is how the meaning of the letters for the word *Pit'dah* can make sense. It doesn't compute to say the serpent's mouth is standing at the door to behold, but if we realize that the letter *tet* also means a humble man bowing before a king, it does.

Another confusing example of the letter ט *tet* is that both the words טהר *tahor* which means clean, or a potential for goodness; and the word טמא *tamei* which means dirty, perverted, impure; begin with a *tet*. It is as if the letter *tet* can represent both good and evil. I think of it as the serpent can test us and we either learn from those tests and become clean, good *tahor* or fail those tests and become unclean, evil *tamei*. Let me clarify that being clean or unclean is not a sin and does not represent good or evil. If a person allows himself to be unclean and continue in impurity it could lead to evil, but my point here is to simply show how the letter ט *tet* is a contranym (its own opposite) with some of the words that it begins with.

Hope you're not confused. If you are keep reading hopefully the next part will make more sense.

Since the stone is about a mouth to behold, I thought of how we can praise Yahuah, how we can give thanks, or how we complain, and profane Him. Interestingly the phonetically same letter of ט *tet,* which makes a *t* sound, is the letter ת *tav*. If the letter *tav* is placed in the word instead of the *tet* for the *t* sound in the word for the *Pit'dah* stone (i.e. we wouldn't change the sound of the word but the spelling), then the word has a *pey* פ meaning mouth; and the rest of the word is *toda* תודה, which means thanks.

The letter ת *tav* means a mark; it is the final Hebrew letter. So, when making the sound of the word, we can choose the snake (placing the letter *tet*) connecting our mouths to the ט *tet,* or we can sound out that word with a letter *tav* ת. Using the letter *tav* connects our mouths to His mark by being thankful and giving Him praise. From the letters and their meanings, I concluded that this stone is to remind us to give up the ways of a twisted, snake-like mouth and turn it to thanksgiving and praise.

The second stone reminds us to be thankful and not to complain.

Jeremiah 33:11 the voice of joy, and the voice of gladness, the voice of the bridegroom and the voice of the bride, the voice of those saying, Praise (Aleph/Tav) Yahweh of Hosts, for Yahweh is good for His mercy endures forever; those who shall bring the sacrifice of thanks-giving into the house of Yahweh. For I will bring back the captivity of the land, as at the first, says Yahweh. Psalm 107:1 Give thanks (hodu **הדו***) to Yahweh, for He is good; for His mercy endures forever.*

הדו ליהוה כי-טוב כי לעולם חסדו

Hodu l'Adonai ki tov, ki la'olam chasdo

Our understanding of what it means to give thanks is most likely a little shallow. The verb for **תודה** *todah* meaning thanks comes from **ידה** *yada* meaning to confess, praise, and to give thanks. In this root, is the word **יד** *yad* for hand. It is probable that the word for thanks originated from *yadad* meaning to cast, as in casting away sins. This includes private and national confession of sin, as seen in *Leviticus 16:21 Then Aaron shall lay his two hands on the head of the living goat, and shall confess (***והתודה** *vahetvada) over it all the iniquities of the sons of Israel and all their transgressions, and all their sins; . . .* from HAW theological Wordbook of the Old Testament this word is partly defined as "to acknowledge or confess sin". This concludes that when we think of being grateful our heart should have some level of repentance, some level of confession, and therefore we are thankful and give praise because we are forgiven. This thought of connecting these two meanings for one word is applied in personal relationships too. How can one word mean both praise and thanksgiving, and also confession of sin; in other words thank you and I am sorry? It has to do with respecting the other. When I admire someone, I am thankful for what they do, and at the same time if I admire someone, I am sorry if I hurt them. Our mouths should be full of praise - admiring what Yahuah does for us and also full of repentance—sorry when we hurt Him. There should not be any bitterness, complaining, or condemnation. In all circumstances we are to be thankful.

1 Thessalonians 5:16-18 Rejoice always, pray without ceasing, in everything give thanks, for this is the will of Elohim in Messiah Yahshua toward you.

As discussed about the letter *tet* there is both good and evil. Ironically Yahuah created both good and evil. We may not understand how that can be; therefore, we need to remember that even if someone is treating us evil, we should be giving thanks to Yahuah. Yahuah created both good and evil, period. Be thankful in all circumstances and remember He is in control. This goes back to having some level of repentance.

Whether in good or evil circumstances we still need to recognize our own failures. When we see our own failures and then we are repentant, we realize what we are and how much we are forgiven and can find strength to be thankful even in difficult situations.

Isaiah 45:7 forming light and creating darkness; making peace, and creating evil: I, Yahweh, do all these things.

Along with the confession, we praise because we are grateful that Yahuah keeps His promises. If we remember that He promises to take care of us and even forgive us, then we should be able to be thankful, even if our situation is difficult.

Being that our mouths can praise or condemn, the main focus for wearing this stone is being thankful, and as defined; that includes a level of confession and repentance. As mentioned, this stone begins with a letter פ peh which represents the mouth. The most common way we either praise with thanksgiving or condemn and complain is through our mouth. This stone of being thankful would not be complete if we didn't mention that we need to hold our tongue and use it for praise instead of complaining. There are so many verses about holding the tongue; it should be something we take great care to be careful.

Philippians 2:12-16 So then, my beloved, even as you always obeyed, not as in my presence only, but now much rather in my absence, work out your salvation with fear and trembling; for it is Elohim who is working in you, both to will and to work for the sake of His good pleasure. Do all things without murmuring and doubtful reasoning; that you may be blameless and harmless, children of Yahweh without fault in the midst of a crooked generation, even having been perverted, among whom you shine as luminaries in the world, holding up the Word of Life, for a boast to me in the day of Messiah, that I ran not in vain, nor labored in vain.

James 5:9 Do not murmur against one another, brothers, that you not be condemned. Behold, the Judge stands before the door.

Before moving on to the next verse, connect this verse to the Hebrew letters for *Pit'dah.* As mentioned, this stone has the letters פ *peh* meaning mouth, ט *tet* meaning serpent, ד *dalet* meaning door, ה *hey* meaning behold. James is mentioning the very character this stone is representing - hold your *peh* mouth, choose *tet* good not evil, because that judgment is at the *dalet* door, seeing if you *hey* behold Yahuah or choose not to.

Ephesians 4:29-31 Let not any evil word go out from your mouth, but words that are useful and good for edification, that it may impart a blessing to those who hear them. And do not grieve the Holy Spirit of Elohim, by whom you were sealed to the day of redemption. Let all bitterness, and anger, and wrath, and tumult, and evil speaking be put away from you, along with all malice.

1 Thessalonians 5:18 In everything give thanks, for this is the will of Elohim in Messiah Yahshua toward you.

James 3:1-12…a tongue can set a forest into flames

Matthew 12:36 But I say to you that every vain word, whatever men may speak, they shall give an account of it in Judgment Day.

Obviously wearing a garment of thanksgiving should include focusing on what Yahshua did for us. This is part of where the confession and repentance and of being thankful comes in. Walk by Yahshua's side, imagine seeing Him being beaten, having thorns pressed into His head, having nails painstakingly hammered through His hands and feet. Imagine every emotional pain of being rejected, being mocked. He suffered more than any of us can imagine and He didn't deserve any of it. Put on this garment of thanksgiving in all circumstances. If we are truly following Him, we should expect some difficulties. *John 15:18-27.*

Can we get to the point that we are thankful for hard times and grateful that He allows us to be in the wilderness? It is in those wilderness times that we get to know Him better, where He dresses us with His garment of praise.

He offers us beautiful garments, even those that might compare to the beauty of the

Lilies.

Isaiah 61:3 to appoint to those who mourn in Zion, to give them beauty instead of ashes, the oil of joy instead of mourning, the mantel of praise instead of a spirit of infirmity, so that one calls them trees of righteousness, the planting of Yahweh, in order to beautify Himself.

Wear the stone of *Pit'dah* choosing good not evil, connecting to being truly grateful. Let this gratefulness be heard through the words of your mouth.

Chapter 6

Applying the Pit'dah פטדה *Stone*

1. How can we get our tongues and even our thoughts (we will focus on thoughts with the next stone) to be thankful instead of complaining? Our gratitude has to be in our heart. Go through each of the situations, and others that may come to mind, that were listed in the *Odem* stone and admit at least one thing for each that you grumble about.

A. Finances

B. Father

C. Mother

D. Spouse

E. Talent/Goal

F. Children

G. Yahshua

2. We quickly criticize the Israelites for complaining in the desert. Put that into perspective. They complained mostly out of fear, not trusting, wanting things their way, self-focus. If we are honest, all of us do this. What is your biggest reason for complaining? Again, look at each of the listed situations, what is the root of your complaint in each? Example finance might be fear, spouse might be self-focus, etc.

3. Think back through the questions for the Odem stone. For every situation think of at least one thing to be thankful for. Example if you are struggling with finances, do you still have food on the table, Give Thanks for the food.

4. Go back through the verses mentioned in this section or one that comes to mind and memorize at least one about being thankful. Also go through verses about one's tongue and memorize at least one about keeping a guard over the tongue.

5. Recall at least one time that you have said something to someone that you wish you could take back. Ask Yahuah to forgive you for your evil tongue.

6. Practice being still – wearing the *Odem* stone and now practice watching our tongue and letting gratefulness pour out instead of complaining – wearing the *Pit'dah* stone.

Chapter 7

ברקת *Bareket Stone*

I slowly approach You always learning to control my tongue.
It still stumbles like a dog gasping for breath it searches for a place
to speak its way, but there is a purpose for that breath and
there is a purpose for every word spoken.
Instead of careless utteration and dribbling drool
I begin to keep my mind focused on You, Yahshua.
You show me what is true, You teach me what is right, You help me
focus on purity, love and admiration. The more I keep my mind on
You, the more You pour down like rain. As I open my mouth
You not only fill my dry ground but You overflow.
Like lighting You reach down and fill me with Your ways, Your
thoughts. You show me the battle that is forever raging.
How the enemy is staging his every move. I must be prepared to
enter the battle at any moment, gasping for every drop of You.
Training for any attack, prepared at any moment. My thoughts must
be focused on Your truth, Your ways, Your excellence so that out of
my mouth speaks Your heart.
In the middle of peaceful training, it seems that out of nowhere a
thought will enter my mind and it can alter my entire mood.
One twisted word from another can send me down a
rollercoaster of trapping thoughts and emotions. Diving over the top
of the incline, then my tongue comes back out gasping for its place.
Next thing I know my thoughts overcome the beautiful closeness

I had to You and the ride tithers forward and backward

as if it will fall off of the track. I grab a hold of the safety bar, I grab You, as the track bursts into pieces seconds after

You clutch me in your arms.

This is the Bareket stone. One that is so filled with Yahshua, that even your thoughts are focused on Him and ready for anything that comes your way. That your body, your mind, is completely surrendered; clutching to your Savior.

The word for this stone is defined as to cast forth like lightning. The letters spell out the following meaning: ב *beit* means house ר *resh* means head, or mind ק *quf* means person ת *tav* means seal – His mark. We can summarize those letters as: that place where our mind has control over our body because we are marked with Him.

There is a man in Scripture named Barak. In Judges 4 and 5, Deborah calls him to fight against Sisera. Sisera was the commander of a huge army of Canaan that had oppressed Israel for 20 years. Can you imagine hearing the words that Deborah said to Barak? "Behold Yahuah, the God of Israel, has commanded, 'Go and march to Mount Tabor, and take with you ten thousand men from the sons of Naphtali and from the sons of Zebulun. I will draw out Sisera…"and give him into your hand." Responding to these words, I think my thoughts would second guess these words. I would probably be asking for a sign to confirm this or to justify how they can't be correct . . . are you sure this was from Yahuah? This would be very scary, it would seem an impossible task, but Barak like lightning says yes. He wants Deborah (the prophetess, whose name means word) to come with him. She says okay but that he won't be the one that gets the honor. I have always thought of this as if he were being punished, but actually I think it is positive in its own way. Barak wasn't concerned if he would get honor, but he wanted the Word with him. Then in Chapter 5 Deborah and Barak celebrate that their enemies perish. Like lightning Barak responded, he kept the Word with him and won the battle. This is what this stone is about, responding like lightning. Having Him so engraved in us that we don't even have to stop to think. This stone reminds us to be so connected to Him that we hold our thoughts captive on Him.

Our thoughts should be like lightning, but we need to remember the enemy acts like lightning too. In Luke 10:18 Yahshua says that He was watching satan fall from heaven like lightning. The enemy prowls around and seeks his prey. He can come in and quickly attack leaving us dumbfounded, not even realizing what just happened. How many times in our life has a simple word changed the entire atmosphere of the room? How many persons have had their lives changed in an instant from some type of trauma? I think if we could see satan fall like lightning, we would take our thoughts more seriously and prepare for battle by keeping our minds fixed on Yahuah.

Remember how Peter denied Yahshua three times. I believe he wanted to stand firm but without thinking he denied him. This is an example of those moments when satan like lightning sneaks in and attacks our thoughts, and, therefore, we fall prey to his schemes.

So maybe satan is compared to lightning, but our Savior, Yahshua; our Elohim, Yahuah has a way of being like lightning.

Daniel 10:6 His body was like the Beryl, and His face looked like ***lightning****. And His eyes were like torches of fire; and His arms and His feet in color like polished copper; and the sound of His words were as the noise of a multitude.*

Psalm 18:9-19 He bowed the heavens also, and came down and darkness was under His feet; and He rode on a cherub and He flew; yea He soared on the wings of the wind; He made darkness His covering, His pavilion all around Him, darkness of waters, thick clouds of the skies. Out of the brightness before Him, His dark clouds passed through, hailstones and coals of fire. Yahweh also thundered in the heavens; And the Highest uttered His voice, hailstones and coals of fire. Yea, He sent out His arrows and scattered them, and ***lightnings*** *He shot out and confounded them. Then the streambeds of waters were seen, and the foundations of the earth were bared at Your rebuke, O Yahweh, at the blast of the breath of Your nostrils. He sent from on high, He took me; He drew me out of many waters. He delivered me from my strong enemy, and from ones hating me; for they were stronger than I. They prevented me in the day of my calamity, but Yahweh was my support. And He brought me out into a broad place; He delivered me, because He delighted in me.*

Ezekiel 21:9-11… A sword, a sword sharpened and also polished! Sharpened to make a slaughter, polished to flash like ***lightning****! Or shall we rejoice, the rod of My son despising every tree? It is given to be polished, that it may be handled; the sword is sharpened and polished, to give it into the hand of the slayer.*

Lightning is quick, without time to think. It is what comes out when we are squeezed. It is that knowing to trust Yahuah, just because, without trying to plan it all out. This lightning reminds us how He can deliver us in an instance, reach down and pull us up out of the miry clay, reach down and let us walk on water; or that He can judge us by His polished sword.

We need to be so focused on Him that in a moment our thoughts turn to Him. In fact, we are so focused on Him that we don't even have to stop and think, He is what pours out.

Like lightning; are the thoughts that race through our minds. Our minds should be focused on becoming the mark and producing others to be marked. Unfortunately, our thoughts are often not something we would want others to hear. When we are put to the test, we often have thoughts that prove we are not trusting in Yahuah. When He calls us to walk out a certain task, we often question Him, lacking in trust. When we are in the midst of an argument or difficulty, we spew out things without thinking. When we are afraid, we let those fears override what we know is true. Our thoughts have to be so stayed on Him that we can trust Him completely; and when we are put to the test, He comes out because the depth of our minds is on Him.

2nd Corinthians 10:5 …and bringing into captivity every thought into the obedience of Messiah.

Proverbs 23:7 For as he thinks within himself, so he is…

Isaiah 26:3 The steadfast mind you will keep in perfect peace because he trusts in You.

Philippians 4:8 Finally brethren, whatever is true, whatever is admirable, whatever is right, whatever is pure, whatever is lovely, whatever is good, if there is any excellence and if anything praise worthy think about such things.

2nd Timothy 1:7 For Yahweh did not give a spirit of cowardice to us, but of power and of love and of good discipline. (a sound mind)

This is where His Truth and Spirit are so deep in us that it is who we are. We trust Him so much that we are like Stephen, while being stoned he could only see Yahshua; like Peter who was willing to dive out of the boat in an instant; like Abraham willing to leave everything in order to obey Him; like Yahshua when the enemy confused Scripture and tempted him He knew how to counter the enemy's deception.

In Ezekiel 21:10 mentioned above, the word for lightning is about a polished sword. The sword is the double-edged Word that quickly divides. Our thoughts need to be fed with the Word constantly so that we can rightly divide truth so that when we are in the middle of a battle, the Word pours out not words of anger or fear, etc.

Today our minds are bombarded with things from TV, radio, telephone, internet, etc. Maybe you've been bombarded with abusive words from a parent, a spouse, a teacher, or someone else. Maybe you bombard yourself with negative thoughts about who you are. How can we overcome the things that enter our minds that are not of Yahuah? Do we take enough time to fill our minds with at least the equal amount of time on

His Word? Do we take time to make sure that we have lined up our thoughts with truth?

I will always cherish a comment my son made to me when he was five. He came running into the kitchen exclaiming "Momma, Momma! I know where the devil lives." "Oh really son, where?" "In the TV". How true. We are constantly struck by influences around us and much more now with the internet than the day my son said that. Can we have the impulse as he did and take heed to what we allow in our minds so that we can line our thoughts up with Yahuah?

I pray we can get control of our minds so that we can stay in the palm of His hand, the place of His blessing.

As you read the next few verses, imagine this lightning being that extremely quick decision, one that happens so fast that it isn't even something that has to be thought about. Imagine Yahuah, like lighting, setting His thoughts on you because you are connected to Him through His word.

Habakkuk 3:11 Sun and moon stood in their places; they went away at the light of Your arrows, at the radiance of Your gleaming (lightning- ברק barak) spear.

Zechariah 9:14 Then Yahweh will appear over them, and His arrow will go out as lightning; and Adonai Yahweh shall blow the ram's horn and shall go forth with the windstorms of the south.

Psalm 97:1-6 Yahweh reigns! Let the earth rejoice; let the multitude of islands be glad. Clouds and darkness are all around Him; righteousness and judgment are the foundation of His throne. A fire goes before Him and burns up His enemies all around. His lightnings lit up the world; the earth saw and trembled. The mountains melted like wax before the face of Yahweh, before the face of Yahweh of the whole earth. The heavens declare His righteousness, and all the peoples have seen His glory.

Matthew 24:27 For just as the lightning comes from the east and flashes even to the west, so will the coming of the Son of Man be.

Remember that He, like lightning, can come in and protect you, save you, destroy your enemy.

Deuteronomy 32:41 If I sharpen My flashing (ברק- barak) sword, and My hand takes hold on justice, I will render vengeance on My adversaries and I will repay those who hate Me.

Also remember that we need to set our thoughts, like lightning, on Him.

Romans 12:2 And be not conformed to this age, but be transformed by the renewing of your mind, in order to prove by you what is the good and pleasing and perfect will of Elohim.

Colossians 3:2 Set your minds on things above, not on earthly things.

Chapter 8

Applying the Bareket ברקת *Stone*

1. In the first 2 stones we discussed disturbances that take away our stillness and troubles that cause us to complain and not be thankful. With this stone I don't want to focus on the influences outside of ourself but on the thoughts that come from within. Many times, we are our own worst enemy. So, with the *Bareket* stone let's focus on the thoughts we condemn ourself with. Think of thoughts you have about yourself. Be honest and list at least 3.

2. Do you have thoughts about not being good enough, not being pretty enough, not achieving enough, being too young, being too old, being unforgivable, etc.? Do you think negative thoughts about who you are to the point that you don't realize how much Yahshua loves you? Is there anything in your past that causes you to think you are too unworthy to receive Yahshua's love? Maybe something you did that you can't seem to forgive yourself for? Maybe something that someone has done to you that continues to beat you up day after day? Maybe someone's words that abuse you over and over? Think of anything that continues to cause you to stay outside of Yahshua's loving embrace and list it now.

3. On the opposite end of this spectrum, we might get a little lofty. Do you ever have thoughts about being better than someone else? Have you seen someone dressed tacky, living as if on the street, and thought negative things about that person? Have you had thoughts that someone should have done things your way, as if saying you are better than they are? Have you judged someone else thinking yourself better? Think of at least 2 times when you have thought of yourself in a prideful way.

4. Line up your thoughts with Scripture.

- Where there are emotions that make you feel unworthy find a verse that reminds you of how much He loves you. Maybe John 3:16.

- In the situations where someone has abused you with negative words remember Yahuah is close to the broken hearted. Maybe Psalm 34:18, Isaiah 54:4.

- When there are moments that you have thought yourself better than others remember to lift others up. Maybe Philippians 2:4, Luke 6:27-28.

5. Continue through your thoughts against yourself, thoughts against others, and thoughts that are too much for yourself and line them up with Scripture. Please be ready to share these verses with others. Memorize at least 2 verses about thoughts or about the actions Yahuah can take that are like lightning.

6. Remember a time when you either said or did something without thinking?

Sometimes we say something or do something that we don't stop to consider how the other person might perceive it or have enough empathy to consider how it might make another person feel. In your experience, recall a time when not stopping to think about the other person's feelings caused that other person pain. Have you asked that person for forgiveness? Ask Yahuah to forgive you, now forgive yourself.

7. Think of a time when someone did or said something to you without thinking how it might make you feel. Did that person apologize later? Have you been able to forgive that circumstance, if not, give it over to Yahuah. If that person has asked for forgiveness, then forgive and let it go. If that person hasn't asked for forgiveness then at least give it to Yahuah and let it go. Trust Yahuah with it. He is a faithful and just.

8. Think of a stressful time or a traumatic time you have experienced. What thoughts, words, or actions came out? Maybe it was a flat tire, maybe it was a life-threatening moment, maybe it was a heated argument. Think of as many times as possible and look back on your ability to – like lightning – focus on Yahshua.

Chapter 9

נפך *Nophek Stone*

Another day passes and I feel I am nothing but a failure. I try to stop and take notice of You, God. I try reading Your Word, singing Your praise, giving You thanks. I try to line up my thoughts with Yours, but truth be told, some days I just feel like I am

going through the motions.

Like the energizer bunny, I busy myself with doing the things I know I am supposed to do but then it comes like a tornado.

There isn't even a tornado horn,
the weather man gives no warning.

There is an incredible sucking wind that grabs me so quickly that I don't even have time to consider fighting it. I am lifted off my busy path and slammed to the ground. I fail You again and know I can't measure up. Shame creeps in and I know I am not worthy to even call out Your name. I hide in a dark corner questioning why I even exist. The blaring sounds of the tornado ripping everything in its path, block out any comfort, I am useless. No matter how hard I try I am one consistent screw up twisting around like a storm of destruction until I blow through my desolate *path and then leave myself as a wasteland. I want to crawl away and simply never exist.*

How can I repair the damage of my sinful errors,

of my careless words? The damage is done, the winds have destroyed everything – everyone in its path.

There is no way to turn back time and make *every moment like a sunny day with a gentle breeze. The damage is done.*

Then You pull me up out of the misery, out of the putrid place of vomit and disgust. You love me no matter what. You truly love me. You give me comfort in those darkest places, even in the places that I have *failed You. Even in those places that seem unchangeable, unforgivable.*

This is the Nophek stone; accepting His love and realizing that even in our fallen state He is willing to scoop us up and clean us up so that He can cherish us in the palm of His hand.

The letters of this stone *Nophek* are **נ** *nun* which represents a resurrected fish, **פ** *peh* representing a mouth, and a **ך** *caf* (soffit form-the soffit form is simply the way 5 of the Hebrew letters are written if they come at the end of a word) representing in His palm. So, we can define the word *Nophek* **נפך** as a person resurrected from self with a mouth that puts that person in His hand, or worded a little better to understand - be one that is resurrected to a place, gathered like a fish in a net to a place of being set apart in the palm of His hand.

I divided this word into the letter for **נ** *nun* for fish, and the remaining letters *peh* and *caf;* which leave the word **פך** *puk.* In Hebrew this word *puk* means a container, a can, as if being set apart and placed in a container. Maybe that container could be like His palm. Our words and thoughts, as we reflected in the stones for *Pit'dah* and *Bareket,* should set us apart, place us in a setting different from the world.

The word פך *puk* is found in Isaiah 54:11.

Isaiah 54:11 . . . our stones will be set in antimony.

The word antimony is *puk*. In other words we will be set apart, separate. I think this is a little different than the word *kadosh* for holy. *Kadosh* also means to set yourself apart. If we walk in His ways, following His ways, keeping Shabbat, keeping the feasts in His ways; we make efforts to set ourself apart, to be Holy. The word *puk* is describing a container – almost as if He is the one doing the action. He takes a container, scoops us out, and separates us, holding us in His hands. Maybe it is that place where we learned to be still by listening for His voice; then we praise Him and are grateful for Him and all He does; then we get our thoughts focused on Him; and now He reaches down and scoops us out, and sets us in antimony.

I think there are two thoughts to consider when wearing this stone. The first one is to truly remember "you are not alone". In Greek, this word for *puk* is *antimonos*. It means not alone. One can translate this as I set your stones in a place where you are not alone.

Matthew 28:20 ". . . teaching them to observe all that I commanded you; and lo, I am with you always, even to the end of the age."

He has given everything to reach down and scoop you up. We already mentioned Psalm 18:9-19 which gives the imagery that He, like lightning, comes quickly to deliver us. He truly loves each and every one of us. I think many times it is hard for us to realize how much He loves us. I know I personally can't seem to forgive myself or even like myself, but He actually does. He loves even me. Many times, we are too busy to take notice. We get distracted, we fail Him and therefore, we can't truly receive His love. We think we have to earn our way back, but He is eager to reach down and pull us out of the miry clay.

Psalm 40:2 He brought me up out of the pit of destruction, out of the miry clay, and He set my feet upon a rock making my footsteps firm.

1 John 3:1 See what manner of love the Father has given us, that we may be called the sons of

Yahweh; who made us. For this reason the world does not know us, because it did not know Him.

There are many verses about Yahuah choosing Israel (those straight with Elohim).

Deuteronomy 7:6-11 For you are a holy people to Yahweh your Elohim; Yahweh your Elohim has chosen you to be His own treasure out of all the people on the face of the earth. Yahweh did not set His love on you or choose you because you were more in number than any people, for you were the fewest of all peoples. But because Yahweh loved you, and because He kept the oath which He swore to your fathers, Yahweh has caused you to go out with a strong hand, and redeemed you from the house of slaves, from the hand of the Pharaoh king of Egypt. Because of this, know that Yahweh your Elohim, He is Elohim the faithful El, keeping the covenant of mercy to those who love Him, and to those who keep His commandments, to a thousand generations; and repaying to his face those who hate Him, to destroy him; He will not delay, He will repay him who hates Him, to his face. And you shall keep the commandments, and the statutes, and the judgments which I am commanding you today, to do them.

It is as if when we begin to wear these stones, He takes notice. We stop to see the color red, in other words we are still enough to notice Him. Then we begin to praise Him and give Him thanks. Then we get our mind focused on Him and He reaches down and pulls us to Him. As we are there, scooped up out of *Mitzraim* (Egypt – tribulation), He teaches us how to live in His ways, and when we love Him we walk in His commands, statutes, judgments.

John 14:15 If you love Me, you will keep My commandments.

He first loved us and scooped us up; now we can love because His love flows through us. He has done His part, and now He is watching to see if we will do ours.

Back to Isaiah 54:11, I love this verse that has this word פוך *puk* in it. As mentioned above, it is translated in English as antimony but hopefully we are getting a perspective on what this word represents. The entire chapter of Isaiah 54 actually fits the stones that we have discussed so far. This entire chapter speaks of the closeness that Yahshua, the bridegroom to His people who are known as His bride, wants to share with us. It is as if we come before Him completely transparent. He wants to be our spouse, someone that we are completely intimate with. He says shout for joy, break forth into joyful shouting and cry aloud. Can you remember, when as a child, you would get so excited about something? Like a baby getting excited over seeing his hands for the first time, or a child seeing a cat or a dog and feeling the softness of its fur when petting it for the first time. Yahshua wants us to be thankful, full of praise, full of that joy when we see Him. Like a little child excited about Him. When was the last time you came running to Him in joyful praise like a child? I pray each of us can get to that place where we let go of all the fences that hold us back from jubilant praise for Him.

Isaiah 54 then goes into verses about not being full of shame nor humiliated; in fact, it says forget those times when you were widowed - alone. For your husband is your Maker, whose name is *Yahuah Za'vaote*; and your redeemer is the Holy One of Israel who is called the God of all the earth. This is like being so close to Him that His mind is in you. His words, His ways, His thoughts are intertwined with you. There is nothing hidden in you from Him. You are transparent and greatly loved. He is your husband, the eternal bridegroom to His people.

As usual in Hebrew there is often more than one way to understand a word. Words can even be a contranym (polar opposite meanings). Another meaning for the word **פך** *puk* is black powder, eye paint. This is the second thought of this stone **נפך** *Nophek*, be sincere don't be fake.

Jeremiah 4:30 And you, o desolate one, what will you do? Although you dress in scarlet, although you decorate yourself with ornaments of gold, although you enlarge your eyes with paint, in vain you make yourself beautiful. Your lovers despise you; they seek your life.

Matthew 12:34 You brood of vipers, how can you, being evil, speak what is good? For the mouth speaks out of that which fills the heart.

Proverbs 4:23 Watch over your heart with all diligence, for from it flows the springs of life.

Proverbs 10:11 The mouth of the righteous is a fountain of life, but the mouth of the wicked conceals violence.

Let's not cover our eyes to make it look like we are set apart, instead be real. Be transparent. *Nophek* is accepting the fact that Yahuah scoops you close to Him and desires to have all of you, completely transparent, the real deal, nothing fake because He deeply loves you.

Chapter 10

Applying the Nophek נפך Stone

1. So far, our jewels in our garment should be ones that are at peace, being still with Yahuah; mouths of praise and thanksgiving; minds focused on Yahuah; and a heart that sets us apart because it is deeply in love with Yahuah. Stop and pause; think through each one of these jewels. What jewels sparkle on your garment so far? Which stones need to be polished? Do you have the ability to sit still in His presence, to feel calm and have your emotions in check? Do you take time to praise and give thanks to Yahuah? Are you grateful even when in the middle of a storm? Can you keep your mind focused on Yahuah even in the middle of a busy day, and do your words and even thoughts, your heart, reflect that you are set apart? Is your heart opened, transparent with grateful praise, at peace to every thought and word being on Yahuah? Do you realize how much He loves you? Are you in love with Him?

2. Read all of Isaiah 54.

A. Think about verses 1-3. Have you been barren? In other words what things in your life do you feel you never bore any fruit? List at least 1, maybe it's marriage, children, ministry, your walk. Trust Yahuah with those things, continue to pray. You may be stretched before you see the fruit but drive your pegs (what you stand for) deep and hold firm.

B. Think about verse 4. What things cause you to fear? What are you afraid of that would make you feel ashamed, humiliated, disgraced? List at least one. Let Yahshua love you. Give those things to Him, He loves you completely even with your faults.

C. Think about verses 5-6. Your redeemer is your husband. When you feel insecure, unloved, betrayed, rejected, abandoned are you able to let Yahshua come in and be the only thing you need during those emotionally difficult times?

D. Think about verses 7-11. When we realize our sinfulness we feel unworthy and look for the next day to be a day of doom. When we walk through storms, especially abusive ones, we begin to believe we deserve to be punished. But Yahshua will have compassion He will set our stones in *puk*, a place where we are not alone.

3. Think about verses 12-17. Do you ever feel you don't deserve His love? Think of reasons why you don't feel loved. Let Him take that from you and reach down and hold you. Let Him scoop you up and hold you in His arms.

Look back to the verse from *Isaiah 54:11 your stones will be set in antimony and your foundations in sapphires.* This verse actually leads us to the next stone – *Sapir*. The *Sapir* stone might be easier to remember because in Hebrew it sounds similar to sapphire.

Chapter 11

ספר *Sapir Stone*

The audition caused me great anxiety because I was in a room of the elite. These persons were talented, they were beautiful.

I didn't know how I could even begin to compare to them, yet here I was competing against them. As I entered onto the stage, the floor seemed to float under my feet. I wasn't sure I could even make it out on stage. There was a Steinway Grand Piano worth more than I could imagine, complete with a beautiful chandelier hanging over it that glistened before me. There was also a menorah sitting on the corner. The stage was laid out with an area for me to dance; there were more musical instruments for me to play; a song for me to sing; a painting for me to paint; a script for me to act.

I was escorted across the room and I was presented to the judges.

But there was only one judge.

He was dressed in royal clothing. I wanted to bow before Him. His eyes were like deep wells filled with love and compassion. I realized in that moment I wasn't competing against others. The only one I need to perform for is the judge. He wants to see me, He was deeply longing to see me. He truly wanted to share His time with me. He wanted me to blossom and be fruitful.

He was giving me my chance to sing my melody to the tune of my choice; to paint my scenery with the colors that move me.

He wanted to see the character that I would decide to perform. He wanted me to dance before Him as if He were dancing with me. As I begin the audition, I realize that He is truly for me. I can have the honor of having the red carpet rolled out before me,

I can lift my head as if I am royalty or

I can succumb to failure and be bumped off the stage.

This is the Sapir stone, living to be written in the script that allows you to walk into that royal position in His heavenly mansion – to be written in His Book.

The word *Sapir* for this stone is the word in Hebrew for book. It is also the verb to count. The letters that spell *Sapir* can be defined from the letters as a support (ס – *samech*), the mouth (פ – *peh*), and the mind (ר – *resh*). This word is probably an Assyrian root or possibly an Akkadian, and in that language it means to set out on a journey. This word is something that supports the things spoken or thought of like a book. It is also a way of recording things, such as one's journey.

Imagine the beauty of being able to write in a book or to keep a record of something, i.e. to count or to put it in a book. Today we take for granted the ability to communicate through writing. Although we barely even write anymore. We can text and even voice text into our devices and quickly be on our way. Years ago, there was not even a developed letter system much less an entire book. Think about how many years went by when a person could not write or keep record of anything. How exciting it would have been to learn to write and be able to communicate. This first phonetic connection became notable with the Semitic alef-bet. At first the only persons in most ancient cultures that could write were the privileged but it is stated that Israel became a people that could read and write even while in Egypt. Israel became like privileged priests.

Exodus 19:4-6 You yourselves have seen what I did to the Egyptians, and how I bore you on eagle's wings and brought you to Myself. Now then, if you will indeed obey My voice and keep My covenant, then you shall be My own possession among all the peoples, for all the earth is Mine; and you shall be to Me a kingdom of priests and a holy nation. These are the words that you shall speak to the sons of Israel.

This stone is one that reminds us that we have a privileged position. He is willing to count us, put us in His book, write us in the palm of His hand.

Isaiah 49:16 Behold, I have inscribed you on the palms of My hands; Your walls are continually before Me.

Wow! We are so privileged. He chooses us as His own, writes us in His hand, and even writes us in His book.

If I were writing a book about myself about my journey, there are many things I would probably not want to write about. Over the years of mistakes, sins, stupidity, attitudes, etc. I would probably desire to cut those things from the story. Imagine you are producing a movie from a book about you, and all of your character is being filmed. Every word is heard, ever facial expression is recorded, every thought is at least hinted to. Yahshua is watching our movie every day, writing out His book and deciding who gets to be in His book. We need to write out our book in a way that we live up to that task.

Ephesians 4:1 Then I, the prisoner of our Master, exhort you to walk worthily of the calling in which you were called.

Colossians 1:9-10 For this cause also, from the day in which we heard, we do not cease praying on your behalf, and asking that you may be filled with the full knowledge of the will of Elohim in all wisdom and spiritual understanding, That you may live a righteous life pleasing to Elohim and bearing fruit in every good work and growing into the full knowledge of Elohim;

If we read Psalm 40 it seems that, David, the writer of Psalm 40 is writing out his story, wanting to be counted in the book.

Psalm 40:1-17 To the chief musician. A Psalm of David. Waiting I have waited Yahweh; and He turned to me and heard my cry. And He drew me up from the pit of tumult, out of the miry clay; He lifted my feet on a rock; He directed my steps. And He put a new song of praise to our Elohim in my mouth; many shall see and shall fear and shall trust in Yahweh. Blessed is the man who sets Yahweh as his trust, and does not turn to the proud, or to those who turn to a lie. Many things have you done, O Yahweh my Elohim; Your works of wonder and Your purposes toward us; there is none to set them in order to You; I will declare and I will speak; they are more than can be counted (**מספר**- *misapir*- note the word *sapir* as in the *Sapir stone).* *Sacrifice and offering You did not desire; But a body You have prepared for Me. You have not asked burnt offering and sin offering. Then I said, "Lo, I come; in the roll (* **ספר**- *sapir) of the Book it is written of me. I delight to do Your will, Oh my Elohim; And Your Torah is within my inmost soul." I have announced righteousness in the great assembly; behold I will not restrain my lips; O Yahweh You know. I have not concealed Your righteousness in my heart; I speak Your faithfulness and Your salvation (Y'shua); I have not hidden Your loving-kindness and Your* *truth from the great assembly. Do not withhold Your tender mercies from me; O Yahweh; let Your loving kindness and Your truth always watch over me. For evils have surrounded me until there is no number* (מספר- *misapir* again note the word *Sapir); my iniquities have taken hold on me and I am not able to look up; they are more than the hairs of my head, and my heart fails me. Be pleased to deliver me, O Yahweh; hasten to my help. Let those seeking my soul to destroy it, be ashamed and humbled together; let those delighting in my evil be driven back and disgraced. Let them be desolate until it is the reward for their shame; for they are saying to me "aha, aha!" Let all who are seeking You be glad in You and always say, May Yahweh be magnified, those loving Your salvation. But I am poor and needy; Yahweh will take thought for me. You are my help and my deliverer; O my Elohim, do not delay.*

The *Sapir* stone is a plea to be written in the book and to live a life worthy of being inscribed into His book. I think the following verses sum it all up.

Exodus 32:33 Yahuah said to Moses "Whoever has sinned against Me, I will blot him out of My book."

Daniel 12:1 Now at that time Michael, the great prince who stands guard over the sons of your people, will arise. There will be a time of distress such as never occurred since there was a nation until that time; and at that time your people, everyone who is found written in the book will be rescued.

Luke 10:20 Nevertheless do not rejoice in this, that the spirits are subject to you, but rejoice that your names are recorded in heaven.

Revelation 3:5 He that overcomes, will thus be clothed in white garments; and I will not erase his name from the Book of Life, and I will confess his name before My Father and before His angels.

Revelation 20:11-15 Then I saw a great white throne and Him who sat upon it, from whose presence earth and heaven fled away, and no place was found for them. And I saw the dead, the great and the small, standing before the throne, and books were opened; and another book was opened, which is the Book of Life; and the dead were judged from the things which were written in the books, according to their deeds. And the sea gave up the dead which were in it, and death and Hades gave up the dead which were in them; and they were judged, every one of them according to their deeds. Then death and Hades were thrown into the lake of fire. This is the second death, the lake of fire. And if anyone's name was not found written in the Book of Life, he was thrown into the lake of fire.

Chapter 12

Applying the Sapir ספר *Stone*

1. Read Romans 2:6, 2nd Corinthians 5:10, Revelation 20:11-15. According to these verses, we will be judged for our deeds. How do we know if our deeds are leading us to a place that is righteous?

2. Fill in the blanks for the following verse: Deuteronomy 6:25 (differs with various translations.) It will be r__________________________ for us when we take heed to do all these c_________________________ before Yahweh our Elohim, as He has c____________________________ us.

How do you define righteousness? What are some things a righteous person does? What things quickly come to mind that you know are not a walk of righteousness and obeying His commands?

3. Yahuah gave us the Torah, the *Nevi'im* (prophets), the *Ketuvim* (writings) and the *Brit Chadashah* (Renewed covenant) so that we would know how to obey His commands. We do not have the ability to do this on our own so Yahshua came to show us how. He came to write these commands on our heart. Jeremiah 31:31-34 explains it well. He has come to write His way in us. It is not just head knowledge trying to walk it out but heart, love, desire, zeal to have His way written within us, to be written in Him. He forgives us and clothes us in righteousness. Think of at least 2 things you are doing that you feel convicted are not righteous.

4. If you were writing a script for your life, what would be the plot? What would be the climax? Maybe there is more than just one climax, list a few if needed. What has been the most pressing conflict or conflicts? How do you want the story to end? If you can write your story out.

5. Go back and read Psalm 40 can you write out a story line? Is there a rising action or conflict? What is the climax? What is the resolution and what leads to that resolution? Fit your story into Psalm 40.

Before we move on to the next stone let's go back to Isaiah 54 and look at some of the words in Hebrew. From Isaiah 54:11-12. (Read each spaced off section, from right to left, in order to read the verse.)

עניה
Oh afflicted one

סערה
storm tossed

לא נחמה
and not comforted,

הנה
behold

אנכי מרביץ
I will set

בפוך
in antimony

אבניך
and your foundations

ויסדתיך
I will lay

בספירים
in sapphires

ושמתי
moreover I will make

כדכד שמשתיך
your battlements of rubies

ושעריך
and your gates

לאבני
of crystal

גבולך וכל אקדח
and your entire wall of

חפץ לאבני
precious stones

Depending on the translation used, it can be difficult to follow what the verse is really saying. The above verse is from the *Hebrew English Bible from the Bible Society in Israel.* Other translations use words such as turquoise, lapis lazuli, color gems, fair colors, I have founded you, carbuncle stones, stones of delight and others; so let's look at the words and the meanings. The breakdown of these words could be something like. . . humbled one **עניה**; one being storm tossed **סערה** ; not being comforted **לא נחמה** ; behold **הנה** ; I embedding **אנכי מרביץ**; in eye paint- or in a container **בפוך**; stones **אבניך** of you; and I lay foundation of you **ויסדתיך**; in sapphires **בספירים**; and I place **ושמתי**; brilliant sunlits of you **כדכד שמשתיך**; and gates of you **ושעריך**; to stones **לאבני**; of kindling **אקדח**; and all of boundary of you **וכל גבולך**; to stones **לאבני**; of delight **חפץ**.

The first word **עניה** *aniyah* translated as humbled one comes from a root meaning to answer, respond, testify, force into submission, afflict, oppress. This may be a person who has been mistreated, even abused, forced into submission, someone afflicted or needy. It can be someone that has been humiliated but is also a word from the root that can mean to sing. This word has *Yah* on the end of the word so the full meaning of it is afflicted by *Yah* or *Yah* has answered. So maybe this is something Yahuah allows in order to test and see where someone's heart is; and/or maybe it is something that has occurred, and now Yahuah is answering that prayer.

סערה *soarah* means storm tossed, rage, it is phonetically connected to the word for hair which can also mean very afraid, he-goat or barley. An entire book could be written to connect all those relations, but I think of it as someone who is being greatly tested to come away from the beastly character within us – like hairy Esau – and making it through the storm.

לא נחמה *lo nuchama* this is someone not comforted. The word for comfort is also the name Noah. This person not comforted can be thought of someone outside the Ark, storm tossed afflicted, not within the comfort of Yahuah's protection.

The next part of the verse "behold I embedding you in a container" begins to show the beautiful mercy of Yahuah. This goes back to the *Nophek* stone. This was the stone in which we discussed the word *puk*. Yahuah is reaching down for this person outside the Ark being storm tossed, in a rage of flooding waters, and scooping him out, saving him.

The verse continues that He will take our stones. The word for stone is **אבן** eben. This can be further broken down into the letter **א** *alef* representing Yahuah and the last 2 letters **בן** *ben* meaning son. *Ben* is also the root for *bana* meaning to build. One thought for the word for stones relates to what we let Yahuah build through us and through our children. The word *oben* (same letters as *eben* but different vowel sound) relates to a potter's wheel in Jeremiah 18:3. Our stones are like the willingness we have to allow Yahuah to shape us and build us, as a potter does, so that we build that same character in our children and grandchildren.

Jeremiah 18:1-12 The word which was to Jeremiah from Yahweh, saying, "Rise up and go down to the potter's house, and there I will cause you to hear My words." Then I went down to the potter's house, and behold, he was working a work on the wheel. And the vessel that he made in clay was ruined in the hand of the potter. So repeating he made it, another vessel, as it seemed good in the potter's eyes to make it. And the word of Yahweh was to me saying, "O house of Israel, can I not do to you as this potter?" says Yahweh. Behold, as the clay in the potter's hand, so are you in My hand, O house of Israel. The instant I speak concerning a nation, and concerning a kingdom, to pluck up, or to break down, or to destroy; if that nation against whom I have spoken will turn from their evil, I will repent of the evil that I thought to do to it. And the instant I speak concerning a nation or concerning a kingdom to build up or to plant it; if it does evil in My eye, not to obey My voice, then I will repent of the good which I had said to do good to it. Now then, please speak to the men of Judah and to those living in Jerusalem, saying, So says Yahweh, Behold I am forming evil against you, and devising a plan against you. Now each one turn from his evil way, and make your ways and your doings good. And they say, It is hopeless! For we will walk after our own thoughts, and we will each one do according to the stubbornness of his evil heart.

Let us not be like evil stones that are actually bricks because we are trying to form things our way; but let us let Yahuah shape us, turning our clay into the vessel he desires - a brilliantly transparent shining stone that follows His way and passes that down to our children.

Back to Isaiah 54. If we are these stones created by His hands, He will set us in the foundation and in the sapphires. The word for foundations comes from the root יסד *yesod. Yesod* is to establish, to ordain, to fix, the foundation, a beginning foundation. This is from the beginning. The Torah is from the beginning it is the foundation since creation. Yahshua is the foundation. Yahshua is the walking breathing obeying Word - Torah.

1st Corinthians 3:11 For no man can lay a foundation other than the one which is laid, which is Yahshua.

John 1:1-5 In the beginning was the Word and the Word was with Elohim, and the Word was Elohim. He was in the beginning with Elohim. All things came into being with Him and apart from Him nothing came into being that has come into being. In Him was life, and the life was the Light of men. The Light shines in the darkness, and the darkness did not comprehend it.

So Yahuah lays us in the foundation that is His Torah, His Word, it is Yahshua. He puts us in a relationship with Yahshua and writes us in the sapphires. He writes us in His book.

As we continue to read Isaiah 54:12, we read that He will give us places that sparkle - brilliant sunlits. כדכד *cadcod* may be related to the root that means a jar כד *kad*. The verb כדד *cadad* means to toil severely. So again we see a word that makes us think of the potter being able to mold the clay. **כידוד** *kidod* means to glow red hot.

שמשתיך *shimshtaek* is from the root for the sun. This sparking brilliant sunlits is as if He shapes us, burning out the impurities and then allowing the "Son" to shine through us.

The next few words **ושעריך לאבני אקדח** *usharaik leavnei eqdach* can be translated as the gates of the stones of kindling. The word for gate **שער** *shaar* comes from the word for hair. This word can mean to be very afraid or a rage or a storm. A gate is the means of controlling what is allowed or not allowed in a walled city. These gates are stones of kindling. The word for kindling **אקדח** *eqdach* can mean to bore. I think of this part as the place where a servant decides to bore his ear to the door or gate if you will to his master's house. He is a stone that has been kindled, bored, marked. He will be guarding the gate and only allowing things of Yahuah to be permitted inside the boundaries.

The last part of verse 12 **גבולך לאבני חפץ** *gevulek leavnei chapetz* is a boundary of stones of delight. The entire wall- all the boundaries He gives us – will be a place of delight. The entire Word, His Torah being the foundation will be the boundaries that bring delight. The stones of the breastplate reflect His character, His love, His obedience. These stones of His character, love and obedience are reflected as we are being set in His book. We are to transparently sparkle without impurities; we are to shine for His glory.

Read Revelation 21.

I don't really know how to explain the depth of what the scripture from Revelation 21 is saying, nor do I think I understand even the surface of it, but I believe it is this image of the bride and the stones He desires to build within her. She is wearing her sparkling breastplate (that is a reflection of Him inside her). The verses from Isaiah 54 show us the bride being adorned by her bridegroom. If we take all of the broken down meanings we discussed from Isaiah 54:11-12 and put these explanations in these 2 verses, it means something like this... "Oh afflicted one, you have been tested, abused and mistreated but I am going to answer you. You have been storm tossed and have battled with the 'Esau' beast within you and like those outside of Noah's ark you have not had any comfort. Behold I am going to place you and the things you are building with your children, in a truthful place. I am going to scoop you up. I am going to teach you my foundations, my truth, my Torah, my Word, my commands and write you in My book; inscribe you in Me and Me in you. I will shape you and burn out any impurities in you so that I can shine through you. I will bring you to the gate where you can choose to allow Me to be your master, boring your ear at my gate so you can hear My voice. I will give you boundaries to keep you where you need to be and to keep the enemy out. These boundaries I give you will be places you build for both you and your children in delight."

Revelation 21 makes me think of His wedding chamber where each foundation is a beautiful stone and also a beautiful character. Remembering that He makes the promises we studied in Isaiah and keeping an image of the future place we will dwell with Him in Revelation 21 helps us to wear the next stone.

Chapter 13

יהלום Yahalam Stone

Day after day the torment is without end.

The betrayal, everyone turned against me; my spouse, the community, loved ones. Nothing I said nor did could convince even my own children to believe me.

There was no one standing on my side.

Where are You God?

I know Your love, I know how you came and drew me out of the sinking mire. I am living my life trying to be on the path that lines up with Your Word. I am writing my script according to Your commands, learning about Your Law, learning about Your mercy but there is a wind that has blown across this great wilderness, striking every corner of my life.

Where are You, why are You forsaking me?

Satan has ripped his talons into my very soul, stripping me of everything I have. I was accused by a pastor that I was master minded by satan and that I was an abomination of desolation.

He stated that my children were victims of my character and that I needed an exorcism over me. What did I do Abba? I disagreed with his judgment on someone and now the gas-lighting is beyond what I can apprehend. Am I such a bad person that I just can't see the evil in me? Why was I ever born? I am running this race daily training even my thoughts. I have strengthened my endurance until I could barely catch my breath. Aching from exhausted muscles I beg my body to take just one more step; fainting from the lack of air, I gasp through tears for one more breath; swimming from confusion I am drowning and can't decipher which direction will lead me to the surface. How can I continue running this race that seems to have no finish line? I am going to drown, I am sucking in water, my eyes begin to bulge, my head is about to explode. I toss through the night and dread the coming of another day. Standing on the razor-sharp edges of nails, I have no strength to carry on. In utter exhaustion I can only allow myself to waste away.

Then I heard Your voice ask me "They called my son Beelzebub, do you think you are better than Him?" Oh my, no Abba, I know I am not better than He is. I know I deserve discipline, I earned consequences; now I see. I am learning to know what Yahshua went through; I am learning to die to myself, to allow You, Abba, to discipline me. As I drift off allowing myself to die to anything that could be an obstacle, the oil begins to flow. It pours out as I am pressed, it pours out of the pain and soothes every open wound.

Somehow the torment ends, I have been pressed and now I am satiated with the ability to shine my light a little brighter, a little stronger, more empathetically and with self-control.

This is wearing the Yahalam stone. It is going through the discipline even when there is no understanding of why it started or when it will end; going through the pressing even when you are at no fault and being used as one falsely accused. It is knowing that this hammering leads to His oil, to His merciful light.

The word *Yahalam* יהלום comes from the root הלם *halam* meaning hammer, or to smite, as in destroying carved works. The letters represent the hand of Yahuah from the letter י *yud;* behold from the letter ה *hey;* the shepherd staff, or tongue from the letter ל *lamed;* a nail or to connect from the letter ו *vav;* and, water from the letter מ *mem.* So this could be summarized as the hand of Yahuah that beholds the shepherd's staff (His tongue) that leads and connects to water. The word means hammer or to smite. Again, looking at the letters and the meanings of those letters it is Yahuah using His tongue - His Word - to lead someone to the water. This truly lines up with the purpose of discipline. Discipline is a pressing of the flesh to destroy the carved works, the selfish ways, the things not of Yahuah.

The following verses have some form of the verb.

Psalm 74:6-7 And now all its carved work they smash (יהלמון *yahalomun*) *with hatchet and hammers. They have burned your sanctuary to the ground; they have defiled the dwelling place of Your name.*

It can refer to the destruction of a cluster of vines. *Isaiah 16:8. For the fields of Heshbon have withered, the vines of Sibmah as well. The lords of the nations have trampled down its choice clusters…* trampled down is the word הלמו *halmu* from the same root of הלם *halam*.

The word for this stone is defined as I will hammer or require hammering.

Proverbs 18:6-7 A fool's lips bring strife, and his mouth calls for blows (למהלמות *l'mahalumot*). *A fool's mouth is his ruin and his lips are the snare of his soul.*

Proverbs 19:29 Judgments are prepared for scoffers, and blows (ומהלמות *umahalumot*) *for the back of fools.* We will be scraped, chiseled, polished up, hammered. When we speak things out of line we will be disciplined.

This stone is one that is humble and willing to be disciplined.

Revelation 3:19 Those whom I love, I reprove and discipline; therefore, be zealous and repent.

Hebrews 12:10-11 For they disciplined us for a short time as seemed best to them, but He disciplines us for our good, so that we may share His holiness. All discipline for the moment seems not to be joyful, but sorrowful; yet to those who have been trained by it afterwards it yields the peaceful fruit of righteousness.

Deuteronomy 8:5-6 And you have known with your heart that as a man disciplines his son, Yahweh your Elohim disciplines you. And you shall keep the commandments of Yahweh your Elohim, to walk in His ways and to fear Him.

1 Corinthians 9:25-27 Everyone who competes in the games exercises self-control in all things. They then do it to receive a perishable wreath, but we are imperishable. Therefore I run in such a way, as not without aim; I box in such a way, as not beating the air; but I discipline my body and make it my slave, so that, after I have preached to others, I myself will not be disqualified.

Some translations of 1 Corinthians 9:27 say "strike my body". My Hebrew *Brit Chadasha* (New Testament) translation uses the word drive נהג *noheg*. Not only does this stone represent a willingness to be disciplined but also a drive to walk things out to learn self-control and have a desire to be corrected so that we can run the race and win. It is like the ones training for the

Olympics. They train and discipline their bodies to perform in a way that they may win the prize.

Desiring discipline is something we should want. Even though it is not pleasant, we know it removes the impurities and strengthens us drawing us closer to our Savior. An athlete would never be able to win the race if he didn't train his body. We have to be trained, disciplined, in order to be prepared.

Discipline is different from abuse. I don't think we should desire abuse or martyrdom, but if we are placed in it we need to have the strength to suffer through it. There are so many stories throughout history when discipline has fallen into a deep level of torture, even martyrdom. One of those who were greatly tortured was a Jewish man that became a believer. His name was Richard Wurmbrand. Richard and his wife were arrested and their son was left homeless although some neighbors risked caring for the child of a prisoner. Richard was greatly abused by Communist torturers. He was in solitary confinement for 3 years and tortured beyond imagination, then in a group cell for 5 years where the torture continued. He suffered much persecution including a box with nails. They would make him stand in the box for hours, even days; they would beat the bottoms of his feet, to the point that he never walked normal again; they would hang him upside down and place him in a freezer. Then when he was almost frozen they would thaw him back out and repeat the process. They beat him, branded him with burning iron, the list goes on and on. He was released but then immediately arrested again and sentenced for 25 more years. He was miraculously released 5 years later. Amazingly, even after all the torture, he and his wife had a quote they shared -- "Hate the evil systems, but love your persecutors. Love their souls, and try to win them for Christ."

So many have been tortured, martyred, only because of their belief. Some have been tortured because they refused to be forced to do something that would not honor Yahuah. A young girl was shot because she refused to spit on a Bible. Some have been grotesquely abused just because of who they are - the Holocaust.

Think about the apostles, leaders of the way. Paul was beheaded. Peter was crucified upside down. Andrew was said to have been crucified. Andrew was stated to have said "I have long desired and expected this happy hour. The cross has been consecrated by the body of Yahshua hanging on it." Thomas was pierced with swords. Phillip was arrested and cruelly put to death. Matthew was stabbed to death. Bartholomew (Nathaniel) was martyred by being flayed with a whip. James was stoned or thrown off a pinnacle of over 100 feet. Simon wouldn't sacrifice to a sun god so he was killed. Matthais (the one chosen to replace Judas Iscariot) was burned, stoned, or beheaded. John was put in boiling oil but escaped unharmed and later isolated on Patmos. Some of these are traditions passed down to how they died and there are traditions for all of them, but they are based on trusty sources. The only documented one in scripture would be for James. *Acts 12:2 And he had James the brother of John put to death with a sword.* We could include Stephen in this list of martyrs and at the very top of our list is Yahshua Himself.

The humbleness of those that have been martyred yet are full of forgiveness, the unselfishness of those that feel unworthy to the point that they actually long for martyrdom, the humility of those that desire to be crucified upside down because they don't feel worthy to die the same way as Yahshua seems an impossible place to be. This stone is that stone that wants to be disciplined and is willing to be broken at any cost.

Our prize is so much more valuable than we can imagine. Shouldn't we expect to need discipline and self-control? Shouldn't we have a desire to be disciplined? Can I say "Yahuah would You discipline, prepare me, get me ready, put oil in my lamp so I can win the race!" If we truly consider the cost, those are not words that are easy to say; but we all know that when we get on the other side of the test it teaches us, shapes us, molds us to be who He desires us to be. Can I ever get to the point that I could say "whatever it takes, even to death if necessary"?

Philippians 2:8 Being found in appearance as a man, He humbled Himself by becoming obedient to the point of death- even death on a cross.

Revelation 2:10 Do not fear what you are about to suffer. Behold, the devil is about to cast some of you into prison, so that you will be tested, and you will have tribulation for ten days. Be faithful until death, and I will give you the crown of life.

Matthew 10:28 "Do not fear those who kill the body but are unable to kill the soul; but rather fear Him who is able to destroy both soul and body in hell."

Matthew 16:24-25 Then Yahshua said to His disciples, "If anyone desires to come after Me, let him deny himself, and let him bear his torture stake, and let him follow Me. For whoever may desire to save his life will lose it. But whoever may lose his life for My sake will find it."

How do we get to the place that we trust Him enough to walk through anything?

Suffering, betrayal, rejection, abuse, imprisonment, starvation, torture are all ways of being tested to the seeming unimaginable. One has to have the Ruach HaKodesh to survive these things. But these tests are the very experience that will produce oil.

Matthew 25:1-13 "Then the kingdom of heaven will be comparable to ten virgins, who took their lamps and went out to meet the bridegroom. Five of them were foolish, and five were prudent. For when the foolish took their lamps, they took no oil with them, but the prudent took oil in flasks along with their lamps. Now while the bridegroom was delaying, they all got drowsy and began to sleep. But at midnight there was a shout, 'Behold, the bridegroom! Come out to meet him.' Then all those virgins rose and trimmed their lamps. The foolish said to the prudent, 'Give us some of your oil, for our lamps are going out.' But the prudent answered, 'No, there will not be enough for us and you too; go instead to the dealers and buy some for yourselves.' And while they were going away to make the purchase, the bridegroom came, and those who were ready went in with him to the wedding feast; and the door was shut. Later the other virgins also came, saying, 'Lord, lord, open up for us.' But He answered, 'Truly I say to you, I do not know you.' Be on alert then, for you do not know the day nor the hour.

There may be many ways to get the oil in our lamp, but one way is definitely through the trials we go through. The ones that have been persecuted, even to the death, definitely received oil in their lamp.

Gethsemane comes from 2 root words. The first one is גת gat. *Gat* is an olive or wine press. This is the place where one is pressed until oil comes out. The second word is from שמן *shemone.* This word is for the number 8. The number eight represents something new; it also means to grow fat such as the fatness of the land but it denotes an overflow of oil. Gethsemane is where Yahshua prayed just before His horrible death. He was showing us what it takes to be able to reflect the *Yahalam* stone; what it takes to be willing to be hammered, disciplined, pressed to the point of releasing oil.

Chapter 14

Applying the Yahalam יהלום *Stone*

1. Think of a time that you have been mistreated. Write down at least one time that you have suffered something that you might consider to be persecution. Even though it is very hard, can you let it go? Do you have the ability to do as Richard Wurmbrand did and pray for your enemy, to pray as Yahshua did "Father, forgive them, for they do not know what they are doing."? Pray that Yahshua will hold you close and help you to let go of any hurt you are holding onto.

2. In 2 Corinthians 12:10 it states ". . . I delight in weaknesses, in insults, in hardships, in persecutions, in difficulties. . ." Why, or it may be better to ask, how could Paul find pleasure in such things? The rest of the verse says ". . . for when I am weak, then I am strong." Go back to some of the ways you have been mistreated, list the ways that those circumstances have made you strong.

3. The Hebrew word for *strong* is חזק *chazaq*. It means to become firm, strong, and courageous. It is one of the words used for the hardening of Pharaoh's heart; it is used in Exodus 3:13 for Yahuah's strong hand. In Psalm 18:1 it is the word used for Yahuah is my strength. How would you define the strength that Paul is referring to in 2 Corinthians 12:10? Have you been able to get that kind of strength from the things you have suffered? Read Psalm 18. Note that this is the Psalm for the day Yahuah delivered David from the hand of all his enemies. Let that type of strength be the strength you receive when mistreated.

4. Memorize at least two verses, or one that you find about persecution, from this section of the *Yahalam* stone.

Matthew 5:10 Blessed are those who are persecuted for the sake of righteousness, for theirs is the kingdom of heaven.

John 15:18 If the world hates you, you know that it has hated Me before it hated you.

Timothy 3:12 Likewise, all those desiring to live a righteous life in Messiah Yahshua will be persecuted.

Romans 8:35 Who shall separate us from the love of Messiah? Shall tribulation, or distress, or persecution, or famine, or nakedness, or danger or sword?

Matthew 5:44 But I say to you, love your enemies and pray for those who persecute you.

Mark 10:29-30 But answering, Yahshua said, Truly I say to you, there is no one who forsook house, or brothers, or sisters, or father, or mother, or children, or lands, for My sake and the good news, that will not receive a hundred-fold now in this time, houses and brothers and sisters and mothers and children, and lands, with persecutions; and in the coming age, eternal life.

Chapter 15

לשם *Leshem Stone*

Paul wrote to us so that we may not sin. Yahshua said go and sin no more. I felt the deep longing to awaken to righteousness, to follow in the steps of the one I was claiming to believe in.

I felt as if I were walking on an unbeaten path to an isolated island. The Scriptures were pouring through my memory . . . whoever abides in Him does not sin;

Whoever sins has neither seen Him nor known Him;

Follow in His steps – He committed no sin;

Don't use grace as an excuse to keep sinning;

Live by the Spirit and put to death the deeds of the body;

Everyone who practices sinning is practicing lawlessness, for sin is lawlessness;

Don't present your body as instruments of unrighteousness to sin, but present yourself to Yahuah as being alive;

Sin shall have no dominion over you;

Be Holy because I am Holy.

It wasn't that I felt like Yahuah would disown me if I weren't obeying every little rule; it is that I want to know Him and want to represent Him as He is.

Over the years I had stopped participating in any of the holidays that weren't of Him.

Halloween was obvious to me; I shouldn't participate. When I read about Valentine's Day I knew I didn't want to be entangled in that either. One by one I felt like Abba was eliminating things from me that did not represent Him. One by one I knew I needed to step away from things of this world. I started homeschooling and tried to teach from the Scriptures in every subject. As I began to walk on these paths different from everyone else, the false accusations were like knives at a circus act. I was the one tied up on a spinning wheel and the ones throwing the daggers were trying to hit me instead of trying to miss me. I could loosen the cords but wanted to follow the Name I am claiming to believe in; so, I had no choice but to continue to let the daggers fly. I needed any dross within me to be removed, I wanted and still want to be pure. I want to look into my Savior's eyes and for Him to be able to see Himself in me.

The daggers kept coming "Oh Miss Righteous, you think you're better than anyone else"; "You're crazy"; "All of your problems in this life are because of you and your religion"; "You're in a cult"; "So do you think everyone is going to hell except you"; "You are so judgmental"; "You have issues"; "God loves people but obviously you don't".

The more I tried to follow the Word, the more I got accused of things that didn't even make sense. I wasn't accusing anyone of anything; I wasn't being a Torah terror; I was simply walking it out the best I could. I was accused of deceiving someone, accused of not being forgiving, accused of judging . . . the list of accusations is too long to list. All I knew was that I wanted to obey my Savior. I want to hear Him and obey Him, love Him.

"If you love Me obey My commands."

Not participating in traditional holidays such as Christmas and Easter not only got the daggers flying but created a wedge that seems to have separated me from others – even my loved ones.

I was isolated.

The little island I found myself standing on didn't have a path to go back. I don't want to go back. The daggers are constantly still thrown, but I don't feel like I am on a spinning wheel, nor do I feel bound by cords. I walk freely in the delight of keeping His commands. I am always learning about how to become more obedient to Him. This isolated island becomes more beautiful every day, and it is less and less isolated. The mockery over kosher eating is almost comical to me now, but I rather enjoy the tropical oasis of coconuts and mangoes growing freely on the trees. I can stop and smell the beautiful flowers. He is constantly showing me more about Him and showing me how to let His name, His way, His character grow inside of me. Now my beautiful oasis is out of reach for the daggers to even come near.

This is the Leshem stone. Going toward Him, wearing His name, letting Him be inside of you.

The simplest definition of this stone, is the word *Leshem*. *Leshem* means to the name, or toward the name. The letters would have the following meanings:

ל *lamed* means a shepherd's staff or tongue

ש *shem* means teeth or something that crushes the enemy to bring peace

מ *mem* means water

The conclusion of the actual letters might mean something like "the tongue or Word that crushes the enemy and leads one to water". This word *Leshem* in Arabic is a verb that means to mark or brand. We are marked with His name. He is the Word that crushes the enemy and leads us to water. He marks us. We are to look, to act, to think, to speak like Him; His Word is in us, He is in us. When we confess that we believe in Him, we are wearing His name. We need to look like His name (His character) so that we don't profane His name, so that we don't profane who He is.

The root of this word **שם** *shem* shows up in the Hebrew word for heaven **שמים** shamayim. Heaven is the place of Yahuah where His name is. The name marks a strong relationship that someone belongs or is owned by. Example a child would be named "the son of ___ or the daughter of ___". One's name reflects where they are in their walk with Yahuah, i.e. the sons of Yahuah. We should realize that names are very important. In fact they are so important that sometimes Yahuah will even change someone's name. Jacob's name was changed to Israel.

Genesis 32:24-30 Then Jacob was left alone, and a Man wrestled with him until the rising of the dawn. And he saw that He had not prevailed against him. And He touched on his hip socket, and Jacob's hip socket was unhinged and he wrestled with Him. And he said, Send Me away, for the dawn has ascended. And he said, I will not let You go unless You bless me. And He said to him, What is your name? And he said, Jacob. And He said, Your name shall no longer be called Jacob, but Israel, because you have struggled with Elohim and with men, and have prevailed."

Genesis 35:9-10 And Elohim appeared to Jacob again when he came out of Padan-aram, and He blessed him. Elohim said to him, Your name is Jacob; your name will not anymore be called Jacob, but Israel will be your name. And He called his name Israel.

Why did Yahuah change Jacob's name? **יעקב** *Jacob* means at the heel of, to supplant, because of, consequence of. It could be worded as "because this occurred (at the heel of something); therefore, this is the consequence." It seems to relate to things at a low point or at the rear.

Genesis 49:19 "As for Gad, raiders shall raid him, But he will raid at their heels. The word for heels is **עקב akav** (the root of Jacob). *Akav* shows a low point.

In *Jeremiah 9:4... because every brother deals craftily...* The word for craftily is **עקוב** akov (again the root of Jacob) shows one dealing craftily or supplanting.

In *Psalm 19:11 Moreover, by them Your servant is warned; in keeping them there is great reward,* the consequence of keeping the commands as a reward is shown. This word for reward or consequences, result is **עקב ekev** (again the root of Jacob).

So what was the name of Jacob really trying to portray? Many focus on the fact that when Jacob was born, he was grasping Esau's heel. Many focus on his name meaning supplanter because Jacob got the birthright from Esau by deceiving him and then deceiving Isaac. But I ask, was he really deceiving Esau? Was he really deceiving Isaac?

Genesis 25:27 . . . Jacob was a peaceful man living in the tents. Jacob was peaceful, plain, a man of the tent. This word for peaceful, plain is תם *tam*. *Tam* means gentle, upright, pious, perfected, complete, ethnically upright.

Psalm 18:26. . . with the pure You show Yourself pure, the word for pure is תמים *tamim.*

Proverbs 11:3 The integrity of the upright will guide them, but the crookedness of the treacherous will destroy them. The word for integrity is תמת *tumat.*

Psalm 18:23 I was also blameless with Him, and I kept myself from my iniquity. The word for blameless is תמים *tamim.*

The meaning of *tam* is similar in meaning to *shalom* meaning peace. In Matthew 5:48 Yahshua tells us to be perfect. One Hebrew word that could be used for perfect is *shalom* another more likely would be *tam*. The Greek word in Matthew 5:48 is *teleios*. *Teleios* is defined as having reached its end, complete in all its parts, mature. This perfection is the same idea as what it means to be *tam*.

Tam is also similar in meaning to ישר *yashar*. *Yashar* means to be level or straight, upright. The name Israel has this root in it. Even in the new name Jacob is given there is some connecting thread to being one of integrity.

Adding even more interest to the word *tam* is that the two stones on the priest's shoulders are the *Urim* and the *Thummim*. *Thummim* is from the root *tam*. So many connections to being one of great integrity, peaceful shalom, upright, straight. It just seems that it doesn't line up with the name Jacob to mean supplanter.

Not to get off on a tangent, but *tam* is phonetically similar to **טמאי** *tamei* meaning unclean. There seems to be a constant twist, a constant thread of deception that the enemy tries to malign our understanding of Scripture. *Tam* means pure, perfect; *tamei* (phonetically similar) means unclean i.e. imperfect. This is just like Jacob's name. Does Jacob mean supplanter, deceiver or does it mean because of or a result of?

Back to the confusion of Jacob's name. This character of *tam* that he is stated to have doesn't line up with the assumed deceptive character that many claim he had. Also, Jacob is one that lived among the tents, implying he studied, focused on the Word. He was not what society defines as a manly man.

In fact Esau was the hunter, the field man, the outdoor woodsy manly-man type. There is nothing stated that portrays Esau as a man of integrity. Jacob was stated to have integrity, and the fact that he lived in the tent and was concerned about the birthright and the blessing alludes to his having a passion for protecting the Word. Esau did not care. He was not forced to give up his birthright. Esau was wanting a blessing but didn't want the responsibility that went with it. Protecting the seed of Abraham now passed to Isaac and now to the next generation seems to be Jacob's passion. Protecting the blessing, the seed - Yahuah's Word, was something Jacob was willing to risk his life for. Even in the dialogue between Isaac and Jacob, there are hints that Jacob was not trying to deceive his father. He wasn't wanting his father to think he was someone he was not, but maybe he was simply trying to convince his father that he had the ability to do what it would take to carry on and protect the seed. It was already told to Rebekah and Isaac that the older would serve the younger. Esau is the one that calls Jacob a deceiver, but could it be that Esau was the deceiver?

Genesis 25:28 states that Isaac loved Esau because he had a taste for game. This verse can be understood to say because he had game in his mouth. In other words because Esau's trickery, game, deception was in Isaac's mouth, Esau was deceiving Isaac to think he would care for the seed.

Joseph was falsely accused; Yahshua was falsely accused. We will be blessed when we are falsely accused. *Matthew 5:11 Blessed are you when people insult you and persecute you, and falsely say all kinds of evil against you because of Me.*

Jacob was called a heel but had the character of being *tam*. So, after striving with man— part of that being overcoming false accusations - and after striving with God, his name becomes one that is straight - Israel. Israel also has the word for *prince* in it. Jacob is no longer the tail but is now the head—the prince. He may have looked weak, he may have seemed to be something that he might have been falsely accused of, but in the end he overcame and held to his character of being *tam*.

We are grafted into Israel. When we take on that name we need to overcome the things that might falsely accuse us. I share the changing of Jacob's name to emphasize that names represent one's character. Yahshua means salvation; Abraham means father of many; Joseph means to increase; Hannah means grace. Every name - especially in Scripture - can tell the story of that person.

Our name can be negative when our character is corruptive. In Ezekiel 23:10 Ohalah was a harlot, her name was considered to be a byword. How many choose the name Ohalah, Jezebel or Haaman or Hitler to name their child? Names represent one's character.

Names are so important that if one was widowed, her brother-in-law would marry her to carry out his brother's name. Deuteronomy 25:6.

A name is one's character, one's legacy passed down to the next generation.

The root word **שם** *shem* from this *Leshem* stone, means name and it also means here. Think of it as "I will write my name here and they will be mine because they act, speak, think, reflect Yahuah."

Jeremiah 31:33 But this shall be the covenant that I will cut with the house of Israel; After those days, declares Yahweh, I will put My Torah in their inward parts, and I will write it on their hearts; and I will be their Elohim, and they shall be My people.

Ezekiel 11:19 And I will give them one heart, and put a new spirit within them. And I will take the heart of stone out of their flesh and give them a heart of flesh.

When we claim to be His we have to look like Him. We have to wear His name and look like His name, His character. The Law shows us how to have His name in (here) in our heart.

My father was a doctor. I have asked others if they needed to have brain surgery would they want to use my dad as their surgeon. Those persons usually give me a questioned look not sure how to answer. Then I explain that my dad was a doctor, but he was a dentist. He wasn't a brain surgeon. He was a doctor, but I can't just put a name on him and give him a different character. We can't just put a label or a title on someone but present them to be something they are not. My Savior is Elohim, but I can't make Him something He is not. How much more important is it that we present Yahshua, Yahuah, for who He is. I can't just call Him Elohim but then present Him as something He is not. He is Sabbath keeping, Feast keeping, Law keeping, grace giving, never changing. He desires for us to wear His name and look like Him, to keep His Law, to walk in His love. We cannot decide Yahshua is something we have just attached a title to; that is what the Israelites did with the golden calf.

This stone is one of going toward His name, not making Him become a name we have created. It is continuing to wear His name even if we are falsely accused. This stone is making sure we don't profane His character.

Isaiah 49:16 Behold I have inscribed you on the palms of My hands; Your walls are continually before Me.

Revelation 14:1 Then I looked, and behold the Lamb was standing on Mount Zion, and with Him one hundred and forty-four thousand, having His name and the name of His Father written on their foreheads.

Revelation 22:4 They (His bond-servants) will see His face and His name will be on their foreheads.

Read 1st John 2:1-29

Chapter 16

Applying the Leshem לשם Stone

1. Think of a time when you have been falsely accused of something. List at least one. Was there any way you could convince others to think what you were being accused of was not true?

Most of the time when we are falsely accused, trying to defend our case only makes us look like the accusation is true. Have you experienced that with anytime you were falsely accused? Have you tried to defend yourself and only been accused of being angry, crazy, argumentative?

2. Being falsely accused usually goes hand and hand with being betrayed. Think of a time when you have been betrayed – maybe in an elementary school friendship, maybe from a co-worker, maybe in marriage. In that time of being betrayed were you accused of something not true? Did you accuse yourself of something not true or begin to question your own integrity? Maybe something on the order of "Am I so bad that I can't even see how horrible I am" or "Yahshua could never love me." Think of any false accusations you have applied to yourself and list them.

3. Jacob fought for his blessing, wouldn't let go. Maybe this was part of what he was battling. He had the birthright and the blessing, but was he questioning his own integrity? He was a *heel* alluding to lowliness. He was born the weaker twin. He was not red, in other words he was not the one with healthy blood flow; he was not covered in hair, in other words he was possibly not fully developed. He had the character and passion for protecting the seed but could he really be a doer, was he strong enough? Was he a deceiver? He held on and fought. Maybe his thoughts were "give me the blessing because although I question myself sometimes, I have the zeal needed to carry this blessing." Think of those times that you have questioned your integrity; ask Yahuah to build you up in what He created you to be; to carry the name He gave you to be.

4. What is your name? What does it mean? Can you find what your name means in Hebrew?

5. Think of things you feel Yahuah has called you to do. How do those things coincide with your name? Are you walking out those things He called you to do?

6. In what ways are you wearing Yahuah's name? In what ways are you profaning Yahuah's name? When we try to make Him someone He is not, we profane, misrepresent who He is. Ask Yahuah to show you who He is and how to wear His name. Profaning His name is a big deal. It is something He will recompense; it is even part of the commandments. We need to represent who He is so that we don't profane His name.

Ezekiel 20:14 But I acted for the sake of My Name, that it should not be profaned in the sight of the nations, before whose sight I had brought them out.

Exodus 20:7 You shall not take the name of Yahweh your Elohim in vain, for Yahweh will not leave unpunished the one who takes His name in vain.

Memorize at least one verse under this section, or another verse that comes to mind about wearing His name.

Chapter 17

שבו Shevu Stone

It was one of the few verses – if not the only verse – I memorized as a child, but it actually became an excuse to live in my sinful nature and be complacent about how I lived my life.

Romans 3:23 All have sinned and fallen short of the glory of God.

I didn't realize it but I was taking that verse to heart and it was weakening my zeal to seek righteousness. Everyone sins, everyone falls, He will give me His grace,

He has covered my sin.

It gave me comfort to know that I am forgiven when I fail.

I was so confident of His grace that it was as if I am forgiven and don't really have to do anything – as if no repentance is even necessary. I didn't realize it, but I was profaning the idea of being holy.

I was living a rather straight walk, not interested in the drug and alcohol scene but also not aware of its dangers. I was a straight A student, over achiever but sin was sneaking its grip on me. I was skipping along on an easy path; the path was wide, smooth, heavily traveled.

When the walk got narrowed I didn't have the passion nor the safety belt to keep me in line.

I stood in front of the snow ski lift waiting for it to lift me up for the first time, I was afraid it would knock me over. Come to find out it was fun, it caught me, carried me to the small incline I was to ski down. My legs dangled in freedom. All I had to do was keep those skis straight and jump off of the chair. With that in mind I would be able to stay in charge – maybe a little wobbly – but I could control it. The lift became fun, entertaining. I sought the next lift going a little higher to the next hill. The ride on the lift was exhilarating. It carried me over hills and valleys, over beautiful scenery. This time getting off the chair was a little more difficult, I stumbled and began to fall but was able to bring myself back in control. I felt my heart race as I made my way back down to the lodge where I began. There were times that my lack of ski experience should have left me limping from a broken leg or crippled, but all was good – actually fun.

I went for the next ski lift.

This time riding on the chair was a rough ride, I wanted off but was too high in the air to be able to jump. As the chair bounced up and down, I felt I could barely see the ground, higher and higher, farther and farther from the lodge it carried me. I thought that the lift would never stop. Finally it dumped me off. It was going so fast that I couldn't even take time to ready my skis, I hit the ground with a thud as the back of the chair hit me. I was afraid, hurting and embarrassed. Then I turned to see the steep drop off before me. How would I ever be able to return to the lodge? What was I thinking? The mountain was so steep that moving forward just a small distance left me hanging, free floating in the air. Someone please catch me. I landed, tumbling through trees and boulders. The scars from this journey would be permanent. God please help me, bring me back to You. Be gracious to me, O God, wash me from my iniquity. I continued tumbling down the hillside. I began to realize that there are rules to follow and consequences to pay; there are temptations to avoid and purity to seek; there is freedom to live and safety to thrive for.

My analogy of the ski trip was my life. Simple things that seemed harmless became large mountains of sinful ways. Actions that left scars on me and on others quickly turned into permanent, undoable sins. O God, how can I turn my face back toward You. I am so ashamed. Purify me, clean my heart. Please Abba, help me leave these scars behind. Restore me to the joy of Your salvation, give me a broken and contrite heart so that I can walk the narrow path staying close to You – facing You – focused only on You. O God, forgive me.

This is the Shevu stone, asking for forgiveness, turning around and going back to His way – to His lodging place.

You may have already heard of the word for this stone in the Hebrew word **תשובה** *teshuvah. Teshuavah* means repent, turn around. **שוב** *shuv* is the verb root. This verb is very frequent in Scripture. It is more than just saying sorry, it is turning around. It is actually going back to something. It is usually in a spiritual return going back to Yahuah. This root is first seen in Genesis 3:19.

Genesis 3:19 By the sweat of your face you will eat bread, till you return **שובך** *shuvcha to the ground, because from it you were taken; for you are dust, and to dust you shall return.*

So why did Yahuah create man? Was it just to bring him from dust to return him to dust. I believe it has to do with the 1-2-1 theory. Example man was 1 then Yahuah saw that it was not good. Most likely because man would be able to do everything his own way. In fact man might get to the point that he would think he was equal to Yahuah. So Yahuah took woman from the side of man, and man was then 2 – incomplete. Then man is to become 1 in marriage and be able to bear fruit. This is similar to our story with Yahuah. He had a place for us to dwell, be one with Him if you will, but then man turned from Him, becoming separated or in essence being 2. Now the bridegroom will return for those that are willing to turn to Him and they will be 1. They will dwell together.

Next this verb root is seen in the story of Noah.

Genesis 8:3 And the water receded **וישבו** *veyashuvu steadily from the earth, and at the end of one hundred and fifty days the water decreased* **ושוב** *vashuv.*

Genesis 8:7 and he sent out a raven and it flew here and there until the water was dried up **ושוב** *vashuv from the earth.*

As you may be beginning to see, it isn't just a turn, as we would do in saying we are sorry; it is returning to something.

Makes me think of an innocent baby. This is where we begin life – basically in innocence. Then we sin, fall away from Yahuah, and now we have to turn back to that state of innocence. We have turned away from Yahuah's ways and need to return to them.

Romans 3:23 All have sinned and fall short of the glory of Yahweh.

Jeremiah 31:1 At that time, says Yahweh, "I will be the Elohim of all the families of Israel and they shall be My people."

Hosea 14:1 O Israel, return to Yahweh your Elohim, for you have fallen by your sin.

The word root **שב** shuv is also defined as restore.

Genesis 28:15 Behold, I am with you and will keep you wherever you go, and will bring you back **והשבתיך** *vahashivoticha to this land; for I will not leave you until I have done what I have promised you.*

When we think of repentance we need to get the full concept of returning to a state of restoration.

Malachi 3:7 From the days of your fathers you have turned aside from My statutes and have not kept them. Return **שובו** *shuvu to Me, and I will return* **ואשובה** *vashuva to you, says Yahweh of Hosts. But you say, 'In what shall we return* **נשוב** *nashuv?' Malachi 3:18 Then you shall return* **שבתם** *shavtim and see the difference between the righteous and the wicked, between him who serves Elohim and him who does not serve Him. Malachi 4:6 He will restore* **השיב** *hashiv the hearts of the fathers to their children and the hearts of the children to their fathers, so that I will not come and smite the land with a curse.*

Looking at the small picture, the Shevu stone reminds us to repent, to turn from our wicked ways and then restore. This pattern of repenting, turning, and restoring can be applied to our daily relationships. When we hurt someone, we need to mend those times and turn back. If we could, we could picture it as turning back time and restoring the relationship back to its origin before there was any hurt, before any wickedness. That would be the perfect image of restoration, but in reality, it would be impossible. There are consequences of our sin that make restoring to the original out of reach. To overcome hurt takes time. To forget what has happened may not ever occur. Not only are the emotions, memories, hurts, disappointments, distrust etc. an obstacle to overcome but the consequences are irreversible.

An extreme example is that of David. His adultery with Bathsheba, murder of Uriah, and the death of their son were irreversible. These consequences could not be restored as if turning back time and forgetting it as if it never happened. This reality triggers a deeper understanding of what returning means.

When Adam and Eve left the garden of Eden 2 cherubim were placed to guard the tree of life.

Genesis 3:24 So He drove the man out; and at the east of the garden of Eden He stationed **ישכן** *yashkan the cherubim and the flaming sword which turned every direction to guard the way to the tree of life.*

The cherubim are seen again in Exodus 25:18. In the Tabernacle, *mishkan* **משכן**, the cherubim adorn the top of the ark. These cherubim seem to have the same role. They are even connected in the Hebrew by the word **שכן** *shakan*. The word *shakan* is actually a word that can mean neighbor, to dwell, to reside, to house, to make settle down. It is as if they are stationed, dwelling, guarding the special place where Yahuah will dwell. They guard the tree of life at the garden and the Torah in the ark. Wisdom and understanding are also called the tree of life in Proverbs 3:18. So in essence they are guarding the place where we can be with Him, which is by following His way - His Torah - with wisdom and understanding.

You may be asking what does this have to do with returning or to do with David and Bathsheba. Think of it this way; when Adam and Eve left the garden it was because they turned away from Yahuah's command. They left the place of being 1 – where Yahuah dwells. When David turned away from Yahuah, the presence of Yahuah left. When we separate ourself from Yahuah (become 2) many consequences occur. As discussed with David and Bathsheba, it is impossible to make things as if one can turn back time, nor can time be turned back to make the consequences disappear in the story of Adam and Eve. This may seem hopeless at this point, but there is a *shuv*, a returning that can still occur. This is where that place the angels guard will become important. When we sin but then truly learn not to ever walk in that path again, we turn away from it, we return to the way of Yahuah. There is a lasting restoration that can occur. Adam and Eve tasted what evil is after they disobeyed. David tasted what evil is after he disobeyed. I doubt that any of them would repeat the same steps if given another chance. If time were turned back as if it never had occurred, they might repeat the same evil because they wouldn't understand the disobedience; but because they know the evil and are truly repentant, they know not to walk in that manner again. They desire to stay in the dwelling place, guarded by angels, where Yahuah dwells.

Yahuah's commands, His Torah, His way, His tree of life is guarded so that when we have fallen off the path we can return and be restored. We can't be restored to our original state but can be restored to a relationship with Yahuah. A relationship in which we desire to follow Him and understand why not to repeat the evils of our past.

Read 2 Samuel 11:1-27. In verse 1 there is already an allusion to this being a test for David to return. The English translation of "in the spring" or "head of the year" is **לתשובת** *litshuvat*. Do you see the root for **שב** *shuv*?

Why the allusion that David needs to return? What has he done? If we look closely, we notice two things about David's character in 1 Samuel 25 in the story with Abigail. Just after Samuel dies, David is angry with Nabal and wants to murder him. He is also confronted by Abigail and the language used between David and Abigail hints to David wanting to marry her. In other words, David seems tempted by the desire to murder and by the desire to commit adultery. Now turn the pages forward to 2 Samuel 11 where David fails by committing adultery with Bathsheba and by the murder of Uriah.

James 1:14-15 But each one is tempted when he is carried away and enticed by his own lust. Then when lust has conceived, it gives birth to sin; and when sin is accomplished, it brings forth death.

So, we have a hint in the Scripture that this need for *shuv* – returning and restoring – is about to occur. We may want to put the blame on Bathsheba, but the culture of the time would suggest that Bathsheba would not have had a choice in saying no to the king. Even so in 2 Samuel 11:4 she returns **ותשב** *vatashav*. Whether she was basically raped or willing, she returns home. There is a hint that her return is with the effort of restoration to her husband because in verse 11:26 and again in 12:15 Bathsheba is not named but instead she is called Uriah's wife, and state that she mourns for Uriah.

David's story is even more pronounced in the fact that it occurs with Bathsheba **בת-שבע**.

Do you recognize the word hidden in the middle of her name? **שב** *shuv*

The name Bathsheba has two root words. The first means daughter **בת** bat. This part of her name comes from the word *son* or to build. It is a person of the home built on the father's instructions. It actually has to do with the word **אבן eben** for stone. Refer to the notes on the *Sapir* stone and the discussion of Isaiah 54. Not only does the word originate from the word for stone, or sons that are being built, but it also resembles the word for house **בית** *beit.* The first part of her name reminds me of 1 Peter 2:5.

1 Peter 2:5 You also as living stones are being built into a spiritual house, a holy priesthood, to offer spiritual sacrifices acceptable to Yahweh through Yahshua Messiah.

The second part of Bathsheba's name includes the root for the *Shevu* stone we are discussing – **שב** *shuv*. The depth of the root of this word is probably too much to discuss but some things to ponder include that it means to take an oath. **שבע** *sheva* is Hebrew for the number 7. Connect the dots of the 7 days of creation, 7 feasts, 7 churches, 7 branches on the menorah, 7th day Shabbat, 7 spirits of Yahuah, all the 7s and the verb of taking an oath. This same root is also the word to satiate, to be full, or satisfied. Bathsheba is one being built to be in the house with the foundation of the 7s being the oath that satisfies. Her very name alludes to the trial David is about to walk through.

If we go back to the story of David and Bathsheba and consider her name and David's hinted character, it still seems to be horrible consequences. These consequences help shape David into becoming someone that can become satisfied on the foundation of keeping the Torah. The consequences are such unfair circumstances to Uriah and the baby. There is nothing that seems fair to them nor to David's family, which seems to fall apart after this incident. But there is something good that can be found when we look at

David's life. I believe we can see that it did change him. Read 2 Samuel 12:18-23. On the 7th day, the day of resting, dwelling with Yahuah, the child dies but David arises, restored. There were many consequences to his entire family because of his sin. He can't turn back time as if it never happened, but he returned and allowed himself to be restored. He moved forward on the right path with Yahuah. Are there any sins of David mentioned after that? I don't know of any that are recorded and I am not saying he didn't but I think his sin of lust and murder were greatly, forever changed.

I am not saying that we will all have to become extreme sinners in order to get right with Yahuah nor should we sin more in order to be forgiven more. I am not saying that once we are greatly tested we will never sin, but I am saying that once we fail, if we will allow ourself to return, turn around and be restored the chances of that sin happening should be greatly reduced, in fact the chances of that sin occurring again should be none.

Luke 7:40-50. . . I suppose the one whom He forgave more. . . Imagine David weeping in Yahuah's presence just as this woman wept at Yahshua's feet, and then on the 7th day he rose up and went and sinned no more.

John 5:14 After these things Yahshua found him in the sanctuary and said to him, "Behold, you are whole again. Do not sin anymore, lest something that is worse than before should happen to you."

John 8:11 And she said, No one, Master. And Yahshua said to her, Neither do I judge you. Go and sin no more.

Truly returning to Yahuah can't erase the past, but it can completely remove any temptation for those sins. Being restored requires that we let go of those things, rise up, overcome them, and dwell with Yahshua. Many will not let themselves return and be restored. Many will carry guilt and shame and not be restored. Think of Judas Iscariot. It is important to not only repent and let Yahuah wash away the sin but also wash away the guilt and shame. The character of shame may be reflected by the person becoming angry, or blaming someone else for every problem, or becoming unsocial. It may result in someone becoming addicted to alcohol or drugs. It may lead to suicide as it did with Judas Iscariot. Don't let sin continue to destroy you because of shame or guilt. Return to Yahuah through Yahshua and be one.

Our verb root of the *Shevu* stone is also similar to **ישב** *yeshev* which means to sit, to remain. And, of course, we should already be reminded of the root for Shabbat meaning to cease, to rest, to put to an end. When we truly repent, return, restore, then we can find Yahuah's rest. Shabbat relates to keeping the Sabbath; but it also relates to the Day of Atonement, Feast of Trumpets, and Sukkot. It is dwelling with Yahuah.

This stone is one of repentance, one of restoration, one of rest. We rest or cease from all distractions, temptations, busyness, and even all of our shame.

Acts 3:19 REPENT **תשובה** *teshuvah and be TURNED* **שובו** *shevu so your sins may be blotted out and times of rest come to you from before the presence of Yahweh.*

Matthew 4:17 . . . **בתשובה** *beteshuvah repent the kingdom of heaven is near.*

Joel 2:13 Yea, tear your heart, and not your robes; and turn to Yahweh your Elohim. For He is gracious and merciful, slow to anger, and of great kindness and He pities concerning the evil.

Chapter 18

Applying the Shevu שבו *Stone*

1. If you could turn back time, what are some things you would not repeat? List at least two and give some explanation as to why you would not repeat them.

2. Most of the time, even if we are truly repentant, it is hard to forgive ourselves. Think on the situations in your life that you would not want to repeat. Do you still hang on to any of those times or have you been able to forgive yourself and move on? After David's baby died, he got up and ate. David was able to somehow let go of the sin, and in his true repentance he got up and did not let the sin of his past destroy the rest of his future.

What sins, errors, stupid words, stupid actions, evil ways, etc. do you still allow to haunt you? If any of these things keep you from rising up and becoming everything that Yahuah created you to be, keep you from being restored, ask Him now to not only forgive you but help you forgive yourself.

3. Look at Psalm 30, before reading it think of the enemy as being the things in the past that were haunting David. Yahuah lifted David from his own enemy of unforgiveness to himself. Now David can sing praise. Even though the weeping over his past and over the death of his son was there, David is able to find joy. This Psalm was sung for the dedication of the house of David. In other words, think back on our comments on this stone . . . coming back to that place where Yahuah dwells.

4. Now that we have thought through the incredible grace Yahuah gives us even for things we have a hard time forgiving ourself for; be willing to give that kind of forgiveness to someone who has a repentant heart about something they did to you. We discussed forgiveness in the application of the *Yahalam* stone. Remember the example of Richard Wurmbrand's willingness to forgive, can you not only forgive, but when someone comes to you in repentance, can you restore?

Think of a time someone has apologized to you and you gave forgiveness. Have you also restored that relationship? This may not seem possible, it may still suffer consequences, but hand it over to Yahuah.

5. Yahshua said "go and sin no more." Once we have fallen short of the glory of Yahuah we are given the chance to be forgiven. When we take that gift of forgiveness we should live our life with our backs to sin. *Teshuvah* repent - turn around face Yahuah and be restored with him. Sin no more! Think of something that keeps pulling you into sin. List it here.

Imagine facing Yahshua. Keep your eyes focused on Him and decide to turn your back to that sin.

6. Let His *Ruach HaKodesh* Holy Spirit blow your way. Turn to Him, let Him restore every part of you, and become one with Him.

7. Memorize at least one verse about returning, sinning no more, washing away the shame, restoring your relationship to the point of refreshing - to the point of rest.

Chapter 19

אחלמה Achalamah Stone

I sit here with the inability to write; I wait because the only one that can explain this stone is the Holy Spirit. My words can't do justice to the beauty of this stone. I relinquish any control so that He can take over my soul. Like the rolling waves He begins to speak, comforting me with the gentleness that rocks me back and forth, sweet whispers through the rushing of the tide; He begins to twirl me around through a field of flowers, fragrances that carry my soul flowing through the presence of lavender, roses, and frankincense to aromas that I can only long for more of. Like the delicate ballerinas of a dandelion, He gently blows and whirls me through the air compassionately guiding me to the place He desires for me to land.

He opens His inner chamber and pulls me into His embrace sharing His deepest thoughts and guiding me in mine. There in His presence, there in His deepest longing, He shows me His secret places, He connects my soul to Him. His oil pours over me like a crashing fountain from head to toe. Oh, the fragrance, I'm in awe.

My body dances as He carries me in His arms through streams of water to a garden of choice fruits, dripping with the sweetness of honey, the sweetness of His words. I surrender all of me, my heart burns with an unquenchable flame. This is the Achalamah stone - intimately connected.

This stone is one of having a deep spiritual connection with Yahuah. If we break down the Hebrew letters, we have **א** *alef* for Elohim, **ח** *chet* for fence, **ל** *lamed* for a shepherd's staff or tongue, **מ** *mem* for water, and **ה** *hey* for behold. If we put those meanings together, we would come up with something like - Elohim guides His sheep with His tongue and places them in a fence where the water is and where they behold Him. I think this truly defines the word because in the middle of this word we find the root **חלם** *chalam*. *Chalam* means dream. It is associated with the root **חול** *chol*. *Chol* means circular motions or writhing in agony; it is used for dancing and for the shuddering of mountains as in during an earthquake. It may seem contrary to define a word as dancing in a circular motion and shuddering and writhing in agony, not to mention that it is also connected with dreaming, but I think we will find a way that these meanings can all be understood together.

Let's look at some places in Scripture where the word or at least the root of the word appears.

There are places where the word is translated as something to do with agony. After the Israelites cross the *Yom Suf* (Red Sea), part of Moshe's song speaks of the anguish that gripped Philistia and Edom.

Exodus 15:12-16 You stretched Your right hand; the earth swallowed them. In Your mercy You led the people whom You redeemed; You guided in Your strength to Your Holy dwelling. Peoples heard; they tremble; trembling **חיל** *chil seized the dwellers of Philistia. Then the chiefs of Edom were terrified* **נבחלו** *nivchalu; leaders of Moab were seized by trembling; all the dwellers of Canaan were melted. Terrors and dread fell on them; by the greatness of Your arm; they are* *silent as a stone, until Your people pass through, O Yahweh, until pass through the people whom You have bought.*

Then just a few verses later we see this verb root used for dancing.

Exodus 15:20 Miriam the prophetess, Aaron's sister, took the timbrel in her hand, and all the women went out after her with timbrels and with dancing **ובמחלת** *uvimcholot.*

In this section of Scripture, it is almost as if the dancing is done because they were not a part of the writhing and agony, but instead they crossed over to being Yahuah's people. In Micah 4:9-10 we again find this root used for agony, but this time it is to the daughter of Zion. Don't worry there is still a hope after the agony.

Micah 4:9-10 Now, why do you cry aloud, an outcry? Is there not a king among you? Has your advisor perished? For pangs **חיל** *chil have seized you like one giving birth? Be in pain* **חולי** *chuli and deliver, Daughter of Zion, like one giving birth. For now you shall go out from the city, and you shall live in the field. And you shall come to Babylon. There you shall be delivered; There Yahweh shall redeem you from the hands of your enemies.*

In both of these Scripture references there is agony, but there is also a victory – a dancing if you will – that comes only because Yahuah chooses to redeem. The beauty of His redemption but also this agony is not something we should forget. There will be times of trouble, times of agony.

Isaiah 21:3-4 For this reason my loins are full of anguish **חלחלה** *chalchalah; pains have seized me like the pains of a woman in labor. I am so bewildered I cannot hear, so terrified I cannot see. My mind reels,* *horror overwhelms me; the twilight I longed for has been turned for me into trembling.*

Nahum 2:10 She is emptied! Yes, she is desolate and waste! Hearts are melting and knees knocking! Also anguish **וחלחלה** *vechalchalah is in the whole body and all their faces are grown pale!*

If we are honest, there are definitely times when fear, or a lack of knowing what is about to happen, can cause us to writhe in agony. There are tragedies and unfair circumstances that occur in our lives. Have you ever had a time when you just cried out maybe even uncontrollably because of fear or because of a loss or an unfair circumstance? Getting on the other side of that, especially in the moment, so that one can dance is part of what this stone is about.

There are other verbs used for dance such as **לכרכר** *lecarcare* when David danced. That verb, **לרקוד** *lerakod – to dance,* is used in 1 Chronicles 15:29, and in Psalm 114:4. But the word for dance with the **חל** *chol* root is found in Jeremiah 31:4, Psalm 149:3-4, and Psalm 30:11

Jeremiah 31:4 Again I will rebuild you and you will be rebuilt, O virgin Israel! Again you will take up your tambourines, and go forth to the dances of the merrymakers.

Psalm 149:3-4 Let them praise His name with the dance; Let them sing praises to Him with timbrel and lyre. For Yahweh takes pleasure in His people; He adorns the humble (afflicted ones) with Y'shua. (salvation)

Psalm 30:11 You turn my mourning into dancing You have loosed my sackcloth and girded me with gladness,

It seems that when this verb is used for dancing it comes after a time of agony. It is as if it is like birthing a child. The pain and agony seem impossible but the joy that comes after is unexplainable. In that moment after the child is born, the mother's focus is for that child. Nothing else matters. I think this is the kind of dance represented; one in which there is a deep whirling connection. Just as a woman in labor has no control of when that will occur, no control of the pain, no control of the length of the labor, etc.; we have no control over the agony moments in our life. In Yahuah's mercy there is a conclusion to the writhing and labor, and in that moment of relief there is a connection that no one can ever take away. This stone is about those moments that we are so deeply connected to Yahuah that there is no way to explain it, no way anyone can take it. Whether it is during the agony, the relief of agony, or a dream; there is a deep swirling, vertiginous, connection.

With that being said, I think this moment of relief after agony shows how to connect dancing with writhing, but let's think more about how that connects to dreams. Just as the labor or times of agony are out of our control, dreams are also out of our control.

Dreams are a way that Yahuah communicates with us. Out of fear of the supernatural, many just write dreams off and ignore them. The truth is that dreams can be a way that Yahuah communicates and we need to learn to listen. Think of the many persons in Scripture that received messages from Yahuah through a dream.

Genesis 20 Abimelech dreams and realizes Sarah is Abraham's wife.

Genesis 28 Jacob dreams about the ladder.

Genesis 37 Joseph dreams 2 dreams.

Genesis 40 The cupbearer and the baker tell their dreams to Joseph.

Genesis 41 Pharaoh dreams and Joseph interprets.

Judges 7 The Midianite and Amalekite armies dream about Israel.

1 Samuel 3 Samuel dreams Yahuah's voice 3 times.

Matthew 1:19, 2:13 Joseph dreams about Mary.

Matthew 27:19 Pilate's Wife dreams about Yahshua.

Acts 9:10 Ananias dreams about Paul.

Acts 16 Paul has a dream about going to Macedonia. 2 Corinthians 12 Paul dreams about heaven.

There are many other places in Scripture about dreams and obviously Yahuah speaks to anyone He desires. Scripture states that He will communicate through dreams.

Numbers 12:6 And He said, Now hear My words, If your prophet is of Yahweh, I will make Myself seen by him in an appearance. I will speak to him in a dream.

Also, don't think of dreams as being a part of the past. Look at how many dreams occurred in the New Testament; besides it is prophesied to happen in the future.

Joel 2:28 "And afterward, I will pour out my Spirit on all people. Your sons and daughters will prophesy, your old men will dream dreams, your young men will see visions.

So hopefully we are seeing a connection between the meanings of dancing, writhing, and dreaming. It is a place that we have no control; it is a supernatural thing. Only Yahuah can make the mountains shudder, only Yahuah can give you the dreams to communicate with you, and I believe in times of agony only Yahuah can get one to the place of dancing again. This stone is a whirling deep connection, a spiritual connection to Yahuah.

Being that this dreamy place is a spiritual connection, let's consider another way our verb root is used. It is used in a way that defines endurance or control. The Pharaoh was a mighty king, and in Exodus 14:4 his army is connected to this verb root. "His army" is called **חילו** *chaylo*. This was something Pharaoh thought he had control over but to Pharaoh's unwillingness to accept, Yahuah was in control. In Genesis 47:6 the Pharaoh tells Joseph to let any mighty man (*enshai chayil* men of might) be in charge of the livestock. He wanted men that could control.

We see this same thought of men that could be in control in Exodus 18:21.

Exodus 18:21 And you, you shall look out men of ability enshai chayil *out of all the people, who fear Elohim, men of truth, hating unjust gain. And you place these over them as rulers of thousands, rulers of hundreds, rulers of fifties, and rulers of tens*.

This perspective of men being in, or that could be in, control is also seen for women. The words used for a woman in control or a woman of ability, one of might is *eshet chayil*.

Ruth 3:11 Now my daughter, do not fear. I will do for you whatever you ask, for all my people in the city know that you are a woman of excellence eshet chayil.

Proverbs 31:10 An Excellent wife eshet chayil, who can find? For her worth is far above jewels.

So dreaming, dancing in the Spirit, having a spiritual excellence, are all ways of connecting with the Spirit of Yahuah. As stated, we have no control of times of agony nor of times of dreaming, but when we let Yahuah redeem us we can have times of dancing and when we connect to Him we are given places of authority. Through His Spirit He will even speak to us in dreams.

Go back and look again at Exodus 18:21, Ruth 3:11, and Proverbs 31:10. All of these mention that these were persons of truth, excellence. Being a dreamer or one that has visions is not something that we have control over, but it is a way that Yahuah likes to communicate. I think our minds can dream things that can deceive us but I know Yahuah gives dreams. He gives dreams to anyone He chooses, but the gift of understanding those dreams, being able to hear Yahuah's voice, taking that message to the next level, is reserved for those that are of excellent character - spiritually connected. Yahuah gives spiritual understanding, spiritual power, spiritual control, if you will; but He wants it to only go to those He can trust.

When someone is given a spiritual gift of being deeply connected, whirled away in the presence of Yahuah, it can become quickly profaned. In other words, a person can become proud and begin to abuse that power. It can turn into witchcraft. The word we have been discussing is **חלם** *chalam*. As discussed, this is the root found in the stone *Achalamah*. Also, we have been looking at roots that include **חל** *chal,* the letters *chet* **ח** and *lamed* **ל**. If we add another **ל** *lamed* to the end of this *chal* root it is **חלל** *challal*. *Challal* means to profane. It doesn't take much to change a word that shows a beautiful intimate connection to a word that destroys, profanes that spiritual connection. Using this deep spiritual connection for one's own power or honor is profanity and deserves an intense level of punishment. In Deuteronomy 13:1-5 those prophets or dreamers that have separated from the presence of Yahuah (counseled rebellion) were to be stoned to death. Yahuah is against false dreamers, against anyone that abuses the Spiritual connection and profanes it.

Jeremiah 29:8 For so says Yahweh of Hosts, the Elohim of Israel: Do not let your prophets and your divining ones in your midst deceive you. And do not listen to the dreams which they dream.

Jeremiah 23:32 Yahweh says, Behold I am against those who prophesy false dreams, and tell them, and cause My people to go astray by their lies, and by their foolishness. Yet I did not send them nor command them. And they will not profit this people at all, says Yahweh.

Unfortunately, the abuse of the spiritual makes most of us hesitant to even try to understand the whirling connection to

Yahuah's Spirit. Maybe that is one reason so many ignore their dreams. There is a fear that it might be this false dream, false spirit, false doctrine instead of something from Yahuah. The beauty of this stone is to learn to let Yahuah be in control and to connect with Him in a deep whirling, dancing, spiritual way. This stone is to connect to His Holy Spirit, to dance with Him, to dream a dream, to let Him be in control, to let loose.

As the days of trouble get closer and closer, I am reminded of the fact that we need to be able to wear this spiritual connection. We need to worship in Spirit and Truth.

John 4:23-24 But an hour is coming, and now is, when the true worshipers will worship the Father in spirit and in truth. For the Father also seeks such, the ones worshiping Him. Elohim is spirit, and the ones worshiping Him must worship in spirit and truth.

There is a spiritual profoundness of Yahuah. He has the ability to show up in a dream or vision which we have no control over, just as He has control over a shaking mountain. This circular dance or storm is something we have to allow Him to be in control of. The dance needs to be one of Him. It is our worship and it has to be about Him. The root we looked at חל *chal,* also means sand. As the *Ruach HaKodesh* Holy Spirit blows on the sand and whirls it in a circle, we have the ability to dance in His spiritual place, we can be one of might in the spiritual place . . . be a dreamer, an interpreter of dreams, one of visions, one that can hear Him without profanity (i.e., without witchcraft – without selfish motives). This is a gift being spiritually connected. This connection can be seen in dreams, interpretations of dreams, visions, spiritual power, or understanding that only comes from Yahuah. This stone is the ability to tune into the voice of Yahuah and comprehend. It is a skill that even though we have no control over it must be developed and carefully kept in line with Yahuah's sovereignty. This stone is that place of dancing with Yahshua, dancing with Yahuah, being inside His fence, dreaming His thoughts, walking in His circular pattern, being near Him because everything has been shaken off and now one can behold Him; a place where we can drink His water or actually let His water run through us.

Chapter 20

Applying the Achalamah אחלמה Stone

1. There are so many places in Scripture that tell of someone's dream or vision. Look at the list mentioned on page 68 and choose at least 2 of those stories or another place in Scripture about a dream and read about it. Does anything catch your attention about the dream?

2. Consider Daniel 2 and the dream of Nebuchadnezzar. The confidence that Daniel had to tell him about the dream and then to interpret that dream is a supernatural connection to Yahuah. When Yahuah speaks to you or to someone you know, do you have the confidence to pay attention to the dream? Next time you have a dream, write it down and ask Yahuah to help you understand what He is communicating to you.

3. Think of dreams that you have had in the past. Write down some of them that you remember. Do you think those dreams were messages from Yahuah? Were you able to interpret those dreams, if so what was your interpretation? How have some of those dreams played out in your life? Write out a chart of the dream, your interpretation, how they have played out.

4. Think of any moments in your life when you have had a "Wow" moment. Maybe it has been in a time of reading Scripture, some moment when you felt Yahuah speaking to you. Remember a vision, or maybe you thought it was just a thought, when Yahuah showed you something. Consider something profound that someone has said to you; who knows maybe an angel spoke to you. Do you think some of those things sound crazy? Do angels really speak to us? Does Yahuah really speak to us through His word or through a dream? Write about at least one incidence. Take time to be in awe that the Creator of the universe has time to stop and speak to you. If you can't remember any times that He has tried to speak to you, make sure you are stopping to listen.

5. Consider at least one time in your life when your emotions have felt out of control, when you felt you were in great agony. Maybe the loss of someone you love, maybe a childhood pet, maybe your first heart break, maybe a time of being abused, maybe something you failed at, maybe an argument, maybe a time you were falsely accused, maybe in giving birth. Those moments consume our every thought. Write down that time and the emotions you dealt with.

Can you take your every thought and let it be focused on Yahshua? Give Him that same amount of focus as you do in moments of agony. Let Him carry you to that place where you only see Him. A place where you dance with Him. A place where you linger and hear His voice, smell His very breath.

6. What are your thoughts on the spiritually supernatural? Does it scare you? Do you hesitate to connect supernaturally to Yahuah? Supernatural spirituality is something that has been profaned, so it is something to have precaution about but don't let fear keep you from the presence of the Holy Spirit. Ask Yahuah to show Himself to you and trust Him to be there with you always.

7. As the end days approach it is so important for us to worship in Spirit and Truth. *John 4:23-24 But an hour is coming, and now is, when the true worshippers will worship the Father in spirit and truth; for such people the Father seeks to be His worshippers. Elohim is spirit, and those who worship Him must worship in spirit and truth."*

Read Habakkuk 3. As you read imagine being spiritually connected to Yahuah, through Yahshua. Look at Habakkuk 3:2 *Yahweh I have heard Your report; I am afraid, Yahweh. Give new life to Your work in the midst of years, in the midst of years make known; in anger remember compassion.* Note that the word for midst is stated twice so pay attention. Midst comes from the word קרב *karav*. This word can mean come near, approach. This prayer from Habakkuk first calls to come near then gives honor to the incredibleness of Yahuah. In verse 10 our word for this *Achalamah* stone shows up when the mountains quake. Habakkuk 3:10 *The mountains saw You and quaked* **ילחילו** *yehilu; the downpour of waters swept by. The deep uttered its voice, it lifted high its hands.* In the conclusion of Chapter 3, verses 17- 19 remind us to stay near to Yahshua, near to Yahuah, in all circumstances. Remember in days of trouble to spiritual connect to Yahuah. Remember to listen to any dreams Yahuah gives you, any visions, any "Wow" readings and linger in those times so that He can speak to you and be with you always.

Before we begin the 4th row of the stones, let's review the 9 we have already discussed…

Odem **אדם** Be still, take notice of Yahuah

Pit'dah **פתדה** Have a thankful mouth, a mouth of praise

Bareket **ברקת** Set your thoughts like lightning on Yahuah

Nophek **נפך** Set apart, scooped into the palm of His hand, line your words with His

Sapir **ספר** Remember you are written in His book, live as if you are

Yahalam **יהלום** Hammered, persecuted, consider the cost

Leshem **לשם** Wear His name without profaning it and wear the name He has given you

Shevu **שבו** Repent and restore

Achalamah **אחלמה** Have a whirling spiritual connection to Yahuah

Looking back over these 9 it seems they have a connection in the fact that they are about how to walk with Yahuah, and that includes everything from being thankful to being persecuted. I look at the last 3 stones as having a connection of being something beautiful or joyful. I connect these last 3 as if they made it to the other side and are walking in Yahuah's spiritual place, shining on His breastplate.

Chapter 21

תרשיש *Tarshish Stone*

One cannot stand on both sides
as the chasm was too wide to cross.

I had to choose the side I want to be on. I emerged from the thicket and tethered on the edge of the summit. Looking down into the deep darkness it seemed impossible. There was a bridge that wobbled with the slightest breeze held to the other side by only a thread.

A pebble slipped from the edge and tumbled so deep that it never sounded its landing.

My soul shook with fear. The path is not for the unclean; it is a path of holiness. With an intense thirst I could hear a deep calling to the depth of my soul. "Cross over!"

I could hear the waters flowing on the other siding
beckoning my name.

As I stepped onto the bridge, tears flowed from within.

To cross over I had to leave everything behind,

I had to let burdens become joy, pride become humility,

brokenness become healing, persecution become strength.

I stepped one step onto the crossing and the narrow bridge creaked, then the thread broke loose and I was falling into the abyss. I know I don't deserve to be satisfied with Your waterfalls but my soul is in despair within me. Then suddenly as on eagle's wings You swooped down to carry me, landing me safely on Your foundation. Your waves and breakers cover me from head to toe with unexplainable joy.

No turning back, crossed over.

This is the Tarshish stone – crossing over into completeness, into joyful peace.

Tarshish comes from the letters ת *tav* which is the last Hebrew letter and means a mark; ר *resh* which represents the head or the start, the summit; ש *shin* which means teeth or a crushing of the enemy; י *yud* which represents Yahuah's hand; and another ש *shin* which again means teeth or a crushing of the enemy. The letter ש *shin*, is the beginning letter for the word *shalom* – which means peace. Looking at the letters I conclude it to be the mark of those humbled who crush the enemy by the hand that crushes. In other words, those who are humble because they have crushed their flesh, and the fact that they have overcome, crushes the plans of the enemy. This stone is that sweet fragrance that occurs when one has overcome and releases a beautiful, pleasing character to Yahuah and to others around.

The letter *tav* ת is added to the beginning of a word when the verb is being put into imperfect tense. This is similar to English future tense. This happens when the subject is for the word *you* in masculine or feminine, both singular and plural; and for the subject when it is *she* or *they* in feminine form. With that being said, we will look for verb roots from the remaining letters of our word.

One of the roots comes from רשש *rashash*. In Persian this word means His Excellency. In Hebrew the meanings related to the verb רשש *rashash* are beat down, shatter, humbled, being willing to pay the cost. *Rashash* appears in Jeremiah 5:15-18.

Jeremiah 5:15-18 Behold, I will bring a nation on you from far away, O house of Israel, declares Yahweh. It is an enduring nation; it is an ancient nation, a nation whose language you do not know, nor understand what they say. Their quiver is like an open grave; they are all mighty men. And they will eat up your harvest and your food, and they will devour your sons and your daughters. They will eat up your flocks and your herds; they will eat up your vines and your fig trees. One shall beat down ירשש *yeroshesh your fortified cities with the sword, those in which you trust. Yet even in those days, declares Yahweh, I will not make a full end with you.*

The root of *rashash* also occurs in Malachi 1:4

Malachi 1:4 If Edom says, We are beaten down, רששנו *rushashnu but we will return and build up the ruined places; so says Yahuah of Hosts; They may build, but I will tear down. And they shall call them the region of wickedness, and the people whom Yahweh is enraged with forever.*

These two verses don't seem to be very joyful but look again at Jeremiah 5. Yahuah is willing to let Israel be crushed, but He promises not to let it be complete destruction. In Malachi, Yahuah crushes Edom and says He will be indignant to them forever. So, there is a difference. One is humbled but Yahuah has made a promise, and He will keep that promise and will not let His people be completely destroyed. Edom is being humbled but continues in the ways of man. Consider that the Hebrew for Adam (mankind) is the same as the Hebrew for Edom. Edom can represent the manly part of a person, and Yahuah will crush that forever. The verb root we are discussing, *rashash*, shows how one is crushed. This almost seems to fall into the same character of the *Yahalam* stone of being hammered and persecuted; but there is more so keep pushing through.

To explain the fullness of this *Tarshish* stone, think about the following stories.

A man named Ben Stern from Poland went through 9 concentration camps. He survived, but his mother, father, and all his siblings did not. Today Mr. Stern shares his home with a young woman whose grandparents were active Nazis. Mr. Stern felt it would be the perfect person for him to share his home so that he can bring his life story to completeness. Instead of holding on to bitterness, anger, fear or any other traumatic emotion he is choosing to release a sweet fragrance. The young woman is working on a degree pertaining to Jewish history.

Another sweet-smelling story comes from another holocaust survivor, Irene Folgel Weiss. Irene was from Czechoslovakia. As a 13-year-old girl that watched her father, mother, and all siblings (except one sister) being ripped away from her side; she remembers asking another prisoner when she would see her family. The fellow prisoner answered "Do you see the smoke? There is your family." Somehow, she overcame this trauma and married, got a degree, had three children, and now speaks of the Holocaust in order to help warn others of things that can happen in life.

More sweet fragrances come from a lady, Eva Kor, who was also a holocaust survivor and was a twin. Many experiments were performed on Eva and her twin sister. She almost died from the experiments, but she knew that if she died, they would kill her sister being her sister would no longer have a twin. She fought through the horrors to live in an effort to keep her sister alive. Thankfully the war ended, and she and her twin sister actually survived. In order to help heal from the trauma, Eva decided to start an organization that helps connect others who had gone through many of the medical experimentations. She began speaking in many places and was asked to come back to Auschwitz to sign a declaration regarding what happened there and that such a thing should never be allowed to happen again. Eva was also asked to bring a Nazi doctor with her. At first, she thought this was mad to make such a request. She remembered a documentary she had been in and that there was a doctor from Auschwitz in that documentary. She contacted him in Germany and he agreed to come. On her way to meet the doctor, at his home, she was extremely frightened. On her arrival he treated her with great respect. She asked him about his memory of the gas chambers, and he said he had nightmares every day of his life. The two of them went to Auschwitz together to sign some documents at the ruins of the gas chambers. She decided she wanted to give Dr. Munch a gift to thank him for coming to Auschwitz to sign the documents. She gave him a "Forgiveness Letter". A friend suggested she also forgive the doctor that did experiments on her, Dr. Mengele. At first, she was adamant that she couldn't do that but then realized she had the power now – not Dr. Mengele. Her power was that she could forgive. As she read the forgiveness letter to Dr. Munch, she realized hate no longer had a grip on her – this is the fragrance of the *Tarshish* stone. All of these holocaust stories and forgiveness stories are incredible examples of the character of becoming a sweet fragrance.

There are many other stories of horrific trauma that have an unforgettable fragrance that occurs when one forgives and not only forgives but acts in love to the ones that harmed them.

Jim Elliot was a missionary to the Huaorani tribes in Ecuador. He spent months reaching out to the tribe. He dropped gifts by airplane and eventually he and his missionary friends thought it would be safe to actually communicate with them. They were wrong. He and all the missionaries with him were slaughtered by the tribe. Shortly after that his wife Elisabeth Elliot spent 2 years living with and witnessing to the very tribe that murdered him. She had an incredible fragrance.

The most profound story of this beautiful fragrance is that of our Savior Yahshua HaMashiach. Slaughtered, beaten, betrayed, mocked, crucified yet He was forgiving even in the process. He was letting off a sweet fragrance while being beaten and mistreated, and at the same time there is not one drop of bitterness, not one drop of hatred, not one drop of anger - only love.

Luke 23:34 And Yahshua said, Father, forgive them, for they do not know what they are doing....

If we continue to break down our word for this *Tarshish* stone we find several related verb roots. Because there is so much that could be said for the verb roots in this word, here is a quick summary. Some of those verb roots include:

- שושן *shushan* - gladness, joy, lily or in ancient times this was sometimes called a sixie because it had 6 petals. This reminds me of Eva Kor's statement that hatred no longer had control of her. She had the power to forgive and now have joy.

- שש *shesh* - 6 or sheen white linen. This makes me think of when man, being the number 6, crushes everything from within him and is then wrapped in white linen. The day of man is 6, just before day 7 which represents being complete.

Matthew 17: 1-2 And after six days, Yahshua took Peter and Jacob and his brother John, and brought them up into a high mountain privately. And He was transfigured before them, and His face shone like the sun, and His clothes became white as light.

Yahshua went from day 6 to day 7 – away from the ways of man and on to the sweet fragrance and excellency. And just some food for thought . . . *Genesis 7:6 Noah was 600 years old when the flood of water came upon the earth*.

- שיש *shayesh*- alabaster, translucent. This reminds me of Matthew 26:6-13 when a woman pours perfume over Yahshua's feet from an alabaster vase. This occurred just before He was crushed. Also of 1Chronicles 29:2 when alabaster is used in Solomon's temple. It is part of the beautiful material used to build Yahuah's dwelling place.

- ישש *yashesh* - aged maybe meaning matured with honor. This is what happens when the words of James occur. *James 1:2-4 consider it pure joy my brothers when you face many trials, knowing that the testing of your faith produces endurance. And let endurance have its perfect result, so that you may be perfect and complete, lacking nothing.* If we have been crushed and then have the ability to overcome with forgiveness and move on from that trauma, we have matured. As Ben Stern stated, we can bring our life's story to completeness.

- **שוש** *sus* and **שיש** *sis* – both have to do with exultation or joy. This is a type of joy that can't be explained. It isn't temporary. *Isaiah 61:10 Rejoicing I will rejoice* **אשיש שוש** *sos asis*- note how the double *shin* **ש** is repeated- *in Yahweh, My soul will exult in my Elohim. For He has clothed me with the wedding garments of Y'shua (salvation); He has put on me the robe of righteousness, even as a bridegroom adorned as a priest with his fancy attire, and as a bride wears her wedding dress.* For Elisabeth Elliot to sit with a tribe of people that murdered her husband and bring them to a relationship with Yahshua is not a joy that can ever be taken from her. She is adorned with jewels.

- *Shushan* **שושן** and *Shoshanim* **ששנים** are found in the introduction of Psalms 45, 60, 69, and 80. It is connected to the word for testimonies and therefore means lily of the testimonies. This opening to these Psalms may simply be the title of a song but it may mean the very thing this stone represents . . . being a sweet-smelling testimony.

Mark Twain must have understood some of the connection between the fragrance of forgiveness and a lily. Mark Twain: "Forgiveness is the fragrance that the violet sheds on the heel that has crushed it."

Not only are there many roots from the **שש** double shin letters, but we can also find words that have the root for 2 other letters we find in this *Tarshish* stone – **ר** *resh* and **ש** *shin;* **רש** *rosh* meaning head, beginning or summit. I think of it as when we let go of all the troubles and all the trials and then go back to the mountain, the summit, the head, the chief. *Tirosh* תירוש means new sweet wine. It represents a fresh harvest of grapes. When this word is used for *yayin* (wine), it never associates with drunkenness and is often a symbol of heavenly attributes, excellency. Think of what happens to grapes; they are squeezed and sweet juice comes out. It parallels our discussion of being crushed until a sweet fragrance comes out.

Genesis 27:28-29 And may Elohim give you of the dew of the heavens, and of the fatness of the earth, and much grain and wine תירש *Tirosh*-new wine. *May the nations serve you, and peoples bow to you; be a ruler to your brothers, and may your mother's sons bow to you, and cursed be those who curse you, and blessed be those who bless you.*

Deuteronomy 7:13 He will love you and bless you and multiply you, He will also bless the fruit of your womb and the fruit of your ground, your grain and your new wine תירשך *Tirosh and your oil, the increase of your herd and the young of your flock, in the land which He swore to your forefathers to give you.*

Imagine this new wine being the beauty after the crushing. Look at Deuteronomy again, the next thing mentioned is the oil. Oil is also something that has been crushed, or pressed out.

Isaiah 62:8 and many other verses mention this sweet wine. It has been crushed and pressed but has not fermented, not become bitter. It is a sweet beautiful flavor, just like the sweet beautiful fragrance of the crushed lily.

Yahshua's discussion of not worrying is a beautiful way to explain the fragrance of this "joyful-lily", "sweet new-wine" stone.

Matthew 6:25-33 Because of this, I say to you, do not be anxious for your soul, what you eat and what you drink, nor for your body, what you put on. Is not life more than the food, and the body than the clothing? Observe the birds of the heaven, that they do not sow, nor do they reap, nor do they gather into barns, yet your heavenly Father feeds them. Do you not rather excel them? And who of you by being anxious can add one cubit to his stature? And why are you anxious about clothing? Consider the lilies of the field how they grow. They do not labor nor do they spin, but I say to you that not even Solomon in all his glory was clothed as one of these. If Yahweh so enrobes the grass of the field, which is today, and is thrown into a furnace tomorrow, will He not much rather you, little faiths? Then do not be anxious, saying, What may we eat? Or what may we drink? Or what may clothe us? For after all these things the nations seek. For your heavenly Father knows that you have need of all these things. But seek first the Kingdom of Yahweh and His righteousness, and all these things will be added to you.

These verses about the "do not worry", "do not be anxious" are probably some we have heard but we only apply them on a surface level. Imagine being crushed as those in the stories above and think through these verses. As you are being humiliated and stripped of your clothing - don't worry; as you are being starved in a prison or in a concentration camp - don't worry; as you are crying out for mercy and don't think you can live a moment longer - don't worry. Just seek His Kingdom.

I want to share one more story to conclude the meaning of this joyfully crushed stone?

This story is about a man named Humberto Noble Alexander. He led prayer services in Cuba. He was imprisoned in 1962 for 22 years, and the lists of his tortures seem unbearable. They are written about in his book, *I Will Die Free*.

I want to share one of his experiences. He had been beaten and then was thrown into a cesspool of human excrement. He tells his story of trying to at least get his feet to stop sliding on the slime. He states that the odor was unbearable and the nausea was just too much. He finally was able to stabilize his feet enough not to drown on the sewage. He cried out, "Please, Lord, save me. I can't stand it any longer! How long can I possibly survive!" Immediately after his prayer a lily plant came up out of the sewage, just beneath his face – a pure white lily. All he could do was focus on that lily, emerging, opening its beautiful petals, releasing its incredible fragrance.

I think of this stone as the one that represents one overcoming persecution or any trial and then releasing a beautiful fragrance, like a lily, of extreme joy. We put on garments of rejoicing because we have been squeezed to the point of a beautiful pleasing aroma. As we remove the man, the 6, out of our life and after we have been broken down, and then if we turn to great joy, we are like a sweet fragrance (adorned like a lily) and we honor His Excellency.

Chapter 22

Applying the Tarshish תרשיש Stone

1. Go back and read Psalm 45, 60, 69, and 80. First imagine that you have been crushed like those in our stories but now you have overcome and are releasing the joyful sweetness that no one can ever take away. Read through these Psalms with that in mind. Think of Humberto Noble Alexander in the cesspool as you read Psalm 69.

2. Sometimes forgiveness doesn't end up in a happily-ever-after reconciled relationship; in fact sometimes it is not meant to even become a relationship.

Deuteronomy 25:17 Remember what Amalek did to you along the way when you came out of Egypt.

2Corinthians 6:14 Do not be bound together with unbelievers for what partnership have righteousness and lawlessness, or what fellowship has light with darkness?

The point is to not let any bitterness grow up in you, let Yahuah be the judge, don't worry. From what relationships in your life have you suffered a difficult trial? Even if that difficult situation has not been reconciled, have you been able to turn your suffering into a sweet fragrance? Write about your trial, maybe it isn't when someone has been cruel to you, maybe it was a difficult time, or the loss of a loved one. Write about joy you have now that you are on the other side of that trial. If you are not on the other side of the trial, can you find a sweet-smelling lily in the midst of it.

3. Not only is there a sweet fragrance we release after we make it through a trial, but Yahuah rejoices in you when you have a testimony of overcoming. Read the following verse and consider the fact that when we overcome, it pleases Yahuah. Psalm 119:14.

4. Read Revelation chapters 1-3. What is something that all 7 churches have in common?

5. Fill out the following chart. (You may need to draw your own on a separate sheet of paper). List the things that each of the churches have overcome. Reflect in your own life on something that represents your struggles as each one of the 7 churches' struggles. There is a basic example of the church of Ephesus written for you. Write each one - have you overcome? If not, figure out how you can. Overcome and become a sweet flavor, squeezed out; a sweet fragrance of a crushed lily—struck down but not destroyed.

EXAMPLE:

CHURCH	The Positives	The Failings	The Overcoming	My Reflection
Ephesus	I know your deeds and your toil and perseverance you can't tolerate evil men and you test those that call themselves apostles. We accept Yahshua, study and work to keep from being confused by deception. We test another believer's fruit.	"I have this against you that you left your first love." We are failing when we become complacent and lose zeal. To allow oneself to just go with the flow.	Overcome by repenting–remembering from where you have fallen, return to that love.	I lose my zeal, don't pray like I should, get complacent. I get confused on how to not tolerate evil men and testing the verses trying to love them. I need to stand on truth.

Ephesus				
Smyrna				
Pergamum				
Thyatira				
Sardis				
Philadelphia				

Laodicea				

6. Memorize at least one verse about overcoming, or being a sweet smelling crushed out sweet fragrance and sweet flavor.

Look back at Psalms 45, 60, 69 and 80. All 4 of these Psalms begin . . . for the conductor, according to the *shoshannim*. We just discussed the word *shoshannim* in the *Tarshish* stone but before we look at the next stone let's look at the word for conductor **מנצח** *menatseach*.

Although this word is referring to those in the Temple that were leading the work in Yahuah's house, i.e., the Levites, it seems to be hinting to much more. The word not only means conductor but also winner, victorious, eternal, to conquer. The root **נצח** *netsach* is a time of being purified and yet conquering in victory, enduring. In Aramaic it can mean "to make brilliant." Leaders that are purified, that have victory, that dazzle in brightness (or in other words that have been through the process) can help lead someone to have victory and find eternal purity. I think of the beginning of each of these Psalms as being for the conductor, one purified, eternally victorious, an overcomer, **מנצח** *menatseach*. These Psalms also say according to the *shoshannim* **ששנים** (joy that comes after the crushing). Maybe the conductors that led these Psalms had been victorious after being crushed and now can lead these Psalms in joy.

At the beginning of Psalm 60 and 80 the word **עדות** *edut* is added. The word **עד** *od* means witness or testimony. It is part of the word *moedim* – meaning appointed times. It is also part of the word *odi* for ornaments. I think of the introduction of these 2 Psalms as saying – "for the leader that has victory in overcoming the crushing with joy and is wearing that testimony" – or wearing that stone, that precious *Tarshish* stone. **נצח** *netsach* (eternal, victory, overcome, conductor) is also the Hebrew word that would be used for overcome in the book of Revelation for the 7 churches we listed for the *Tarshish* stone.

As mentioned at the introduction of the *Tarshish* stone, the last three stones seem to have some allusion to being crossed over, being the joyful, shining bride. See if you agree as we begin the next stone.

Chapter 23

שהם *Shoham Stone*

Standing in a dry desert I am not thirsty, facing an oncoming storm I have no anxiety, face to face with my attacker I have no fear. All I can see is the glory around me; I am literally filled to overflowing, completely satisfied in my soul.

Stretching myself as wide I can possibly reach,

I lean my head back and open my mouth, I open my heart. I surrender every part of me.

His water gushes through me. I have no longing for anything else, no earthly sustenance, no relationship, no success, no approval, no addiction, no food, no drink – nothing can satisfy me like the deep waters pouring through me.

Covered in a cloak of light and stretching across the heavens His beam from His upper chambers penetrate the waters flowing through me. His clouds surround me like a chariot taking me away on the wings of the wind.

His streams flow through the valleys of my heart and over the mountains quenching my every need. The gentle breeze caresses my face embracing my very being and lifts me into a place of worship. I feel Him inside of me, I feel Him covering me.

Let my meditation be pleasing to You. Let my worship bring honor to You.

I have no emptiness within me; it is completely
satisfied with Him.

Let me go up to Your presence.
I will sing unto Yahuah as long as I live.

I sing praises to my God to the lover of my soul.

This is the Shoham stone, being filled completely with Yahshua.

There is no need for any type of addiction,
or any emotional fulfillment.

He is flowing His Spirit shining
His light to every little corner of one's being.

When we break down the letters of this stone we have ש *shin* that means teeth. Because the word *shalom*, meaning peace, begins with this letter, I usually think of it as teeth that chew up the enemy, crush the fleshy nature so that one can die to self and have peace, *shalom*. A dear friend of mine added more to that thought about teeth. Teeth are used to chew. So maybe we can put these two thoughts together and realize that the way we crush the enemy out of our flesh is by chewing the Word. I think that is a way to think of this letter especially while considering the meaning for this stone. To chew on the Word, i.e., to fill up on the presence of Yahshua, and that will crush the enemy so that we are filled with Yahuah, filled with Yahshua, filled with His peace.

The second letter *Shoham* stone is the ה *hey*. The letter ה *hey*, has the meaning of behold or look; it is the value of the number 5; therefore, it represents both grace and Torah; it also makes the breathy *h* sound and alludes to Yahuah's breath, His *Ruach*

(Spirit). When Yahuah changed Sarah's and Abraham's names, He did so by adding a *hey*. The *hey* reflects the 5 senses and even what are considered to be the 5 levels of one's soul:

1. *Nefesh* = instincts
2. *Ruach* = emotions
3. *Neshamah* = mind
4. *Chayah* = transcendence
5. *Yechidah* = oneness

I don't want to get all mystical about this letter, but I just want to point out that the *hey* is a deep and divine connection to the Holy Spirit (*Ruach HaKodesh*) of Yahuah. This letter *hey* appears two times in Yahuah's sacred name. I think that is a strong hint that it has a deep connection to Him.

The last letter in the *Shoham* stone is the מ *mem*. This is the letter that represents water. It has the value of 40. Think of the many places in Scripture and nature that have a story about the number 40. Noah in the ark, Moshe fasting on the mountain, Yahshua fasting in the wilderness. There are 40 weeks of gestation and many other connections to the number 40. Water is that place that things flow. This water is actually connected to our speech.

Proverbs 18:4. The words of a man's mouth are deep waters; the fountain of wisdom is a bubbling brook.

Water is something we can't live without, yet it can destroy – as in a hurricane. Yahshua gives living water.

John 4:13-14 Yahshua answered and said to her, Everyone drinking of this water will thirst again; but everyone who drinks from the waters that I give to him will not thirst forever. But those waters that I give to him will become in him a spring of water that will spring up into life that is eternal.

This water can flow within us.

John 7:37-38. Now on the High day, which is the last of the feast, Yahshua was standing and He cried out and said, If a man thirsts, let him come to Me and drink. Anyone who believes in Me, as the Scriptures have said, rivers of living water will flow from his belly.

Water droplets will bond into one larger molecule when put close to each other. I think of our connection with Yahshua and with other like-minded believers. We become one, inseparable, flowing stream.

Put the meanings of the three letters of the *Shoham* stone together and it could be defined as a place where the enemy has been crushed by the Word, and now the Holy presence of Yahuah resides there and flows like water making it *echad* (one).

We discussed the word **שם** *shem* in the discussion of the *Leshem* stone. In that discussion we noted that the word *shem* represents the word for name. It is part of the word for heaven and also the word *here.* Another word that has this letter combination in it is very important to understand. The word is **שמע** *shema.*

The *Shema* is the summary, the main focus, of daily and morning prayers. It is the first prayer one learns and the final prayer at one's death. It comes from Deuteronomy 6:4 Deuteronomy *6:4 Hear, O Israel, Yahweh our Elohim is Yahweh echad.*

The *Shema* is sung before Shabbat services, as the last prayer at the Yom Kippur service, at one's death, and many other times. It is usually sung and then there is a pause to consider that this is a blessing so the following words are then sung: Blessed is the name of His glorious kingdom forever and ever. After this part of the prayer, the *ve'ahavta* is sung. The *ve'ahavta* is from the verses Deuteronomy 6:5-9.

Deuteronomy 6:5-9 You shall love Yahweh your Elohim with all your heart and with all your soul and with all your might. And these Words which I am commanding you today shall be on your heart. You shall diligently teach them to your sons, and shall speak of them as you sit in your house, and as you walk in the way, and as you are lying down, and as you are rising up. And you shall bind them as a sign on your hand; and they shall be for frontlets between your eyes. And you shall write them on the doorposts of your house, and on your gates.

The prayer actually continues to Deuteronomy 11:13-21, which speaks of obeying the commandments, loving Yahuah with all one's heart, serving Him and then He will give rain and many other blessings. Are you starting to see a connection to crushing out the enemy and receiving water? The crushing comes from internalizing His Word and obeying His commands and then He sends His rain, His water.

The last part of the *Shema* comes from Numbers 15:37-41. These verses are about the *tzittziot*. The *tzittziot* are the tassels on the corners of garments. The *tzittziot* are a reminder to observe Yahuah's commandments, to be holy to Yahuah.

Let's recall the things we learned about the *Leshem* stone. It was wearing the name He gave us but even more importantly wearing His name. The *Shema* is a good summary of wearing His name. It is obeying His commandments. In fact, the word *Shema* means to hear and to obey. Think of the *Shoham* stone as the *Shema* with the letter *hey* in the middle of it. As mentioned above, that is as if saying let the Holy Spirit (*Ruach HaKodesh*) be in you as you eat the Word and follow His commands so that you can connect to His living water. Come thirst no more.

The *Shoham* stone is not only the stone that was one of the stones embedded on the *Choshen Mishpat* breastplate, but it is also the stone chosen to be used for the *Urim* and the *Thummim*.

*Shemot (Exodus) 28:9 You shall take two onyx (**שהם** Shoham) stones and engrave on them the names of the sons of Israel.*

There were 6 tribes written on one of the *Urim* and *Thummim* stones and 6 tribes written on the other. The understanding of these stones has stumped scholars. The 2 words *Urim* and *Thummim* have been translated many ways. Some say they mean curse and blessing; others say they mean dark and light. If we look at the Hebrew, *Urim* means lights and *Thummim* means perfections. There is a mystical divination that many associate with these stones. The stone is a form of quartz that can develop electrical potential in the minerals. This electrical charge could cause the stone to glow. Many believe the stones changed colors - bright and clear to cloudy and dull. The difficult part of understanding these stones is that the stones seemed to be used in practice of divination or magic. It is something to be aware of because many cultures have similar practices. Egyptian mummies have been found with dice or stones around their necks.

Egypt had *ra* and *thmei* engraved on the breastplate of their god, Hierophant.

Babylonian seers had *urtu* and *tamitu* which was thought to be an oracle from a god.

Islamic Arabs used 2 rods and would draw one out to decide command or prohibition. Ramses III made a breastplate called the *uta* inlaid with precious stones. *Uta* was denoted as the eye meaning to speak. Joseph Smith, founder of Mormon and Latter Day Saints, claims he had *Urim* and *Thummim* and used them as a medium. It seems as if other cultures were trying to emanate the powers that the Israelites had, and obviously the enemy tried to copy it because the names and actions of these other cultures are very similar to Yahuah's way. It always seems – or actually is – the enemies' plan to try to mix the things of Yahuah and the things of the world.

Using divination, turning to mediums, is forbidden in Scripture.

Leviticus 20:6 As for the person who turns to mediums and to spiritists, to play the harlot after them, I will also set My face against that person and will cut him off from among his people.

Deuteronomy 18:9-14 When you come to the land which Yahweh your Elohim is giving to you, you shall not learn to do according the hateful acts of those nations. There shall not be found in you one who passes his son or his daughter through the fire, one who uses divination, an observer of clouds, or one fortune-telling, or a spell caster, or a magic charmer, or one consulting spirits, or a wizard, or one communicating with the dead. For all doing these things is an abomination to Yahweh. And because of these filthy acts Yahweh your Elohim is expelling these nations before you. You shall be perfect with Yahweh your Elohim. For these nations, whom you shall expel listen to observers of clouds (those that practice witchcraft) *and to those divining. But as to you, Yahweh your Elohim has not given to you to do so.*

This gets even more confusing because the role of someone that is a seer is seen in both a positive and negative light throughout Scripture.

It seems positive in *2 Samuel 24:11 And David rose up in the morning; and the Word of Yahweh came to Gad the prophet, David's seer, saying,*

It seems negative in *1Samuel 28:7 Then Saul said to his servants, "Seek for me a woman who is a medium, that I may go to her and inquire of her." And his servants said to him, "Behold, there is a woman who is a medium at En-dor."*

The words for seer and or medium are different Hebrew words in these 2 verses, but it still leads to confusion especially in the English translations. Even more confusing is that even with all these prohibitions and the positive comments and negative comments about seers or spiritists, the priest is told to wear these stones. In fact, we see the Israelites using the stones for answers.

Ezra 2:63 The governor said to them that they should not eat from the most Holy things until a priest stood up with the Urim and Thummim.

Numbers 27:21 And he shall stand before Eleazar the priest, who shall ask for him according to the judgment of the Urim before Yahweh. At his mouth they shall go out, and at his mouth they shall come in, he and all the sons of Israel with him, even all the congregation.

Deuteronomy 33:8 Of Levi he said, "Let your Thummim and your Urim belong to your godly man, whom you proved at Massah, with whom you contended at the waters of Meribah;

So what is the purpose of these *Urim* and *Thummim* stones? Maybe these stones were simply placed behind the breastplate to keep the tribes of Israel close to the heart; after all, the names of the tribes are written on the stones. Maybe the definition of divination, seer, prophet, medium, etc. are not clear. One thing for sure is that part of the confusion of divination is the difference of seeking Yahuah's Spirit instead of some other entity.

Isaiah 8:19 When they say to you, Seek to the mediums and to fortunetellers who peep and mutter; should not a people seek to its Elohim, rather than for the living to seek to the dead?

Whether Yahuah allowed these *Urim* and *Thummim* to light in some way that helped the priests make decisions is not really the question at hand. The question is whom is one seeking. This *Shoham* stone has the *hey* in the middle of the word for name. Seeking His name and letting the *Ruach HaKodesh* speak is how these stones should be understood.

So, getting back to the *Shoham* stone on the *Choshen Mishpat* (breastplate); the letters used in this stone can be rearranged to *mem, shin, hey* which spells *Moshe* (Moses). When considering the walk of Moshe, he represents the Torah – the instructions. One way the letters can be arranged should remind us of the *Shema* that we discussed earlier – hear and obey. The letters can also be arranged as *hey, shin, mem* this spells *Hashem. HaShem* means The Name. In other words name. If the letters are left in the order of the *Shoham* stone, *shin, hey, mem;* they are an acronym for the Psalms of ascent, *Shir Ha Ma'alot.* The Shir Ha Ma'alot are Psalms 120-134. These Psalms represent one's ascent to Jerusalem. All of these letter arrangements and the acronym seem to fit with what this stone portrays – hearing the voice of the Ruach, obeying the Torah, wearing His Name, and ascending to His presence.

Some other word roots that are found in the word *Shoham* include the following:

המה *chamah* = noise unrest, strong feelings. It is noisy. **חם** *chum*= heat, hot, sexual excitation, heat from the sun, rage, anger.

In Genesis 24:21. Rebekah and the servant meet. He watches her in silence, gazes at her actions, waits to see what her true identity is. I think of the root words relating to the *Shoham* stone as a reminder that He is watching us silently. He sees every thought, word, deed, and even every emotion. He will attach peace to our uncontrolled, hot emotions. He does this by silently watching us to see if we will come to the water and draw from its well. This is the part of the bride's garment that digs deep into the spirit and truth, bringing up the water of life and feeding even the camels. This is for those that Shema, those that hear and obey and become one. This is the stone only the bride reflects. It is when the *Ruach HaKodesh* lives inside the bride, inside the ones that have the name written on them.

Again, I think of the last three stones, *Shoham* being one of them, as being one that has crossed over. This one is representing being spiritually connected to *HaShem* (the name, His name). This may remind us of the *Leshem* stone (wearing His name), and it may remind us of the *Achalamah* stone (having a whirling, dreamy connection); but I think this stone is one that has crossed over and is worn by the bride.

My sheep know my voice. She hears His voice when He whispers "Hey – my bride." He has silently watched her as she has come to the well seeking for water and she has sparkled as bridal material.

John 10:27 My sheep hear My voice, and I know them, and they follow Me;

Isaiah 12:3 Therefore you will joyously draw water from the springs of salvation.

Chapter 24

Applying the שהם *Shoham Stone*

1. Read John 4:7-26. What similarities do you see between this woman coming to the well and Rebekah at the well in Genesis 24:10-27? What differences?

Read John 4: 27- 45. What did the Samaritan woman do after she met Yahshua? When Rebekah was willing to feed the camels, it can be thought of as her willingness to give water to others; somewhat like feeding the sheep. With that thought in mind, and with the fact that the Samaritan woman led others to Yahshua, what could be one characteristic of someone that comes to the water and becomes the bride?

2. In your opinion what is the difference between a prophet and a seer; between seer and a medium? The word for prophet in Hebrew is **נבא** *nava* – it means to announce, to utter, to

proclaim, to inform. One of the words for seer in Hebrew is ראה *ra'ah* – it means to look at, to take notice, to understand, to see, a prophetic vision. A word used for a medium as in 1 Samuel 28:7 is בעלת-אוב *baalat ohv* – it means to exercise dominion over, ownership involving communication with the dead.

Considering the difference in these words, do you think there are still persons today that might be prophets? If so, is this a good thing or bad thing?

Consider 1Corinthians 14:1-5; Some have the gift of prophecy.

Consider the word for seer, do you think there are seers today? Could this be a positive thing or a bad thing?

Consider the words of Joel 2:28; How about the word for a medium or spiritists? Do you think there are spiritists today? If so, is this good or bad?

Consider the spiritists in the New Testament from Acts 16:16-18. Since there are false prophets, Matthew 7:15, and since there is so much confusion on the definitions of the different words that represent someone with a spiritual connection, how can we keep our guard up but at the same time not miss out on a spiritual relationship with a spiritual God?

3. What could the *Urim* and the *Thummim* be today? Since Yahuah desires for us to come to Him for answers as stated in Isaiah 55:6 (seek me while I can be found); how are we supposed to get answers today without a tangible answer we can see? Do you think it is okay to ask for a sign to help get a definite answer from Yahuah?

4. Yahuah says My sheep know My voice. Do you ever question if you are hearing clearly from His voice? Think of a time when you asked Him to confirm something you were asking Him. Write about that time. How did He answer you? Frequently He may answer by showing a Word in Scripture, sometimes He may show you a sign. Compare the way He has answered you in times of needing a clear answer to when the Israelites asked for a sign on the *Urim* and *Thummim*. Does that

help you consider that the *Urim* and *Thummim* were not some mystical, magical event, or does it confirm to you that it was mystical? So many things that Yahuah has planned for good have been turned into something not of Yahuah. Think of how the many cultures have something similar to *Urim* and *Thummim*. What things today have profaned the original use of *Urim* and *Thummim*?

5. What sin do you think can quickly tempt someone who might have spiritual power of something similar to the *Urim* and the *Thummim*? What are some ways that persons are tempted today to have a power similar to *Urim* and *Thummim*?

6. Read Jeremiah 29:13. Could this be part of the answer of how to hear His voice? Read the *Shema* from Deuteronomy 6:4-5. Read the following verses and consider that when we are seeking Yahuah we should be seeking Him with all our heart, soul, mind and strength; then we will be able to know His voice. Read the following verses:

2nd Chronicles 15:2; Psalm 34:4; Psalm 37:4; Psalm 63:1-8; Psalm 105:1-5; Psalm 119:2; Isaiah 55:6; Matthew 7:7

7. Consider again that this stone is one where you are silently being watched with His voice whispering His breath to you; letting His water flow through you. Are you bridal material? Can you hear His voice?

8. Memorize at least 2 verses from this section on the *Shoham* stone.

Chapter 25

ישפה Yashphey Stone

For one of my trips to Israel, I was given the incredible opportunity of getting to stay there for several weeks. I knew that Yahuah had a special plan for me. I felt that He planned to redeem me. While I was there, He took each of my painful memories and brought soothing oil to each one.

He spoke to my deep longings in broken relationships, He erased abusive words that had been spoken to me from others, He turned my mourning into dancing.

For the things I missed or couldn't change He filled me with new chances. He lifted my head from my shame and told me to be the beautiful bride He created me to be. I was walking in so much disgrace that I had no desire to wear any of the jewelry that I owned.

Instead of wanting to hold my head up and look like His,

I wanted to hide in a corner. He showed me that He wants me to put on beautiful garments. He wants me to stand beside Him as His bride ready to stand in a position of royalty. Like a beautiful bride He adorned me with oils and perfumes for my hair and skin, He took me to a boutique and dressed me in beautiful linen.

It was so incredible. I actually went to a store and the store owner chose a white dress covered in pearls.

It was modest in every way and covered me completely.

I felt beautiful.

Yahuah was completing me, making me ready to be His bride.

I am by no means complete but He gave me a glimpse of what it should feel like to be His.

If I am His I need to look like the valuable person He considers me to be.

He began covering me with His ornaments – hence this book about the beautiful stones.

This is the Yashphey stone; being beautifully adorned with His oils, linen, jewels, His commandments, His ways and walking as the beautiful bride. A bride completely His, a royal awe-striking bride that holds her head up in a royal position yet has no pride other than the pride she has for her bridegroom.

The last stone on the *Choshen Mishpat* contains the following letters: י *yod* meaning hand, it is usually thought of as Yahuah's hand. Some interesting things about this letter include that it has the value of 10. The plagues of Egypt were completed with the 10th plague. Ten means completion or perfection but includes some level of human responsibility. There are 10 commandments, 10 generations between Adam and Noah,

10 generations between Noah and Abraham, 10 Days of Awe between

Yom Teruah (Feast of Trumpets) and *Yom Kippur* (Day of Atonement). The 10th part in Leviticus 27:32 states that you shall be Holy for Yahuah.

This letter *yod* meaning hand is significant in the 2 verses below. There is a very small letter י *yod* in Deuteronomy 32:17 and an enlarged letter י *yod* in Numbers 14:17.

Deuteronomy 32:17-18 They sacrificed to demons who were not Eloha, to Elohim whom they did not know, new ones who came lately. Your fathers had not dreaded them. The Rock that begat you, and forgot the El who formed you. (begat is ילדך *yeladecha* The first letter is a *yod* and in the Hebrew Scripts it is written very small*)*. This small *yod* could imply that when we forget Yahuah He withdraws His hand.

Numbers 14:17-18 And now, I beg You, let the power of Yahweh be great, as You have spoken, saying, Yahweh is slow to anger and of great mercy, bearing away iniquity and transgressions; and by no means will clear the guilty, visiting the iniquity of the fathers on the sons on the third and on the fourth generation. (Great is יגדל *yegadol*. The first letter is again a *yod* and in the Hebrew Script it is written very large). This large *yod* reminds us that Yahuah's power is great. Notice that power seems to be abundant in loving kindness.

The next letter in this stone *Yashphey* is the ש *shin*. We have already discussed this letter. It means teeth and can represent crushing the enemy to lead to peace or chewing as in chewing on the Word to find truth. This letter has a value of 300. It is the letter used to represent the signature of Yahuah. The number 300 is the number 3 magnified by 100. The number 3 represents the resurrection. The first mention of the number 300 in Scripture is from *Genesis 5:22 . . . And Enoch walked with God three hundred years after he became the father of Methuselah . . .*

The third letter is the פ *pey*. We have also discussed this letter and it means a mouth. It relates to things that are open. It is thought of as the opening that brings things into being. When Yahuah spoke, He brought creation into being. Our words also create things into being. This letter has the value of 80. Moses was 80 when he began to challenge Pharaoh; Ehud was judge for 80 years. Ehud was a warrior in ancient Israel, and was victorious over the Moabites. In Psalm 90:9-10 the life span of man may be 80 years.

The last letter of the Yashphey stone is the ה *hey*. We have also already discussed this letter meaning to behold. It is like the breath or the *Ruach HaKodesh*. The letter *hey* has a value of 5.

Putting the meanings of each letter together, we can define this word something like the hand of Yahuah crushes the enemy and brings peace by showing one to eat the Word so that when one opens his mouth he beholds and the Holy Spirit comes out. This rough summary makes me think of many verses from the book of Revelation.

Revelation 4:5-11 And out of the throne come forth lightning and thunders and voices. And seven lamps of fire are burning before the throne, which are the seven Spirits of Elohim; and a sea of glass was before the throne, like crystal. And in the midst of the throne and around the throne were four living creatures, full of eyes before and behind. The first living creature was like a lion; and the second living creature like a calf; and the third living creature having a face like a man, and the fourth living creature like an eagle flying. And the four living creatures, each one had six wings around, and within being full of eyes; And they had no rest day and night, saying, "Holy, holy, holy, Master Yahweh Almighty, Who was, and is, and is to come." And whenever the living creatures shall give glory and honor and thanks to the One sitting on the throne, to the One living forever, the twenty-four elders fall down before Him sitting on the throne; and they will worship the One living to the ages of the ages, and will throw their crowns before the throne, saying, Master Elohim, You are worthy to receive the glory and the honor and the power, because You created all things, and through Your will they exist and were created.

Revelation 5:9-12 And they sing a new song, saying, Worthy are You to receive the scroll, and to open its seals; because You were slain, and by Your blood purchased them to Elohim out of every tribe and tongue and people and nation, and made them to be kings and priests to our Elohim; and they shall reign on the earth. And I saw, and I heard a sound of many cherubs around the throne, and the living creatures, and the elders, and their number was ten thousand times ten thousand and thousands of thousands, saying with a great voice, Worthy is the Lamb having been slain to receive the power and riches and wisdom and strength and honor and glory and blessing.

Revelation 7:9-12 After these things I saw, and behold, a great crowd which no one was able to number them, out of every nation, even tribes and peoples and tongues, standing in front of the throne and before the Lamb, having been clothed with white robes, and in their hands palm branches. And they cry with a great voice, saying, Salvation to our Elohim sitting on the throne, and to the Lamb. And all the cherubs and of the elders and of the four living creatures stood around the throne. And they fell before the throne on their faces and worshiped Yahweh, saying: Amen! Blessing and glory and wisdom and thanksgiving and honor and power and strength, be to our Elohim forever and ever. Amen.

You can also find similar verses in Revelation 11:16; 14:3; and 15:2-4. All these verses and more are about worshipping around Yahuah's throne. For one to truly worship around the throne, that person has been sifted out; or as we put it in the summary of our letters, the enemy has been crushed by the chewing of the Word. And now that person has the breath of the *Ruach HaKodesh* (Holy Spirit) coming from his mouth, beholding Yahuah. The bride is ready.

Revelation 19:6-7 And I heard as a sound of a numerous crowd, and as a sound of many waters, and as a sound of many thunders, saying, HalleluYah! Because Yahweh, Elohim, Almighty reigns. Let us rejoice and let us exult and we will give glory to Him, because the marriage of the Lamb came and His wife prepared herself.

In conclusion, looking at the letters of this last stone seems to have something to do with worshipping at the throne of heaven. This can also be supported by gematria and by finding this stone in some verses that have to do with the throne. Every Hebrew letter has a numerical value. The gematria of a word is done by adding the value of the letters. If we add all the letter values of word *Yashphey* it equals 395. Interestingly the sum of the letters for the Hebrew word **השמים** *HaShamayim,* which means The Heavens, is also 395.

Some verses that have this word for the *Yashphey* stone in them include the following:

Revelation 4:3 And He who was sitting was like a jasper (**ישפה** *Yashphey) stone and a sardius in appearance; and there was a rainbow around the throne like an emerald in appearance.*

Revelation 21:18 The material of the wall was jasper (**ישפה** *Yashphey) and the city was pure gold, like clear glass.*

As stated, when we studied the *Tarshish* and *Shoham* stones, these last 3 stones seem to have to do with the ones that have crossed over. The *Tarshish* stone shines on those that overcome and let out a joyful sweet fragrance; the *Shoham* stone glistens on those that have the *Ruach HaKodesh*; and the last stone, the *Yashphey*, radiates royalty to those that are worshipping around the throne.

In order to look a little deeper into this word, we could simply break this word into two.

We would get the words **יש** *yesh* which means there is and **פה** *pey* which means mouth.

That could be a very simple way to look at what we worship around the throne . . . "there is a mouth." In other words, there is one that is, that was, and that will always be who is the one that spoke with His mouth things into being.

The *Yashphey* stone contains the word root **שפה** *shaphey* which means to shine.

*Isaiah 13:2 Lift up (***נשפה** *neshaphey) a standard on the bare hill, raise your voice to them. Wave the hand that they may enter the doors of the nobles.*

"Lift up a standard" is to have an extreme shine. **שפת** *shephat* = to set on fire.

Isaiah 26:11-15… 11 O Yahweh, Your hand is high; they do not see; they see and are ashamed of the zeal of the people. Yea, the fire of Your foes devours them. 12 Yahweh, You will ordain peace for us; for You have worked all our works for us. 13 Yahweh our Elohim, masters beside You have governed us; only in You we will mention Your name. 14 Dead ones do not live; departed spirits do not rise; because of this You visited and destroyed them, and caused all memory of them to perish. 15 You have added to the nation, Yahweh; You have added to the nation, You are glorified; You have extended it to the ends of the earth.

In verse 12 the word *ordain*, sometimes translated as establish, is **שפת** *shephat* "you will establish (set on fire) "; in verse 15 the phonetically similar word **שפת** saphat is used twice "you have increased/have added." This word used for to increase or to add is spelled with the Hebrew letter **ס** *samekh* instead of the letter **ש** *shin,* but it is phonetically related to the root *shephat.*

If we look at some word root meanings of **שפת** (shephat) and the phonetically related roots of **ספת** *saphat*, we find that these roots have a connection that describes aspects of the same idea. Some of these roots and meanings are the following:

סף *sap* means threshold, goblet or a based bowl. The threshold is like that border between the two realms of something. It relates to meaning to reach through the border of two realms. Think of it as two circles, one is larger than the other and the smaller one is inside the larger like a wheel in a wheel or like the Holy of Holies in the Holy Place or like a fence around a house.

סוף *sup* or *suf* means to come to an end or a reed. The reeds at *Yom Suf* (the Reed Sea) mark the place where land comes to an end and then there is water. The reed marks the border or edge. Looking back at the previous root of a threshold, can you see the connection?

ספה *sapa* means to snatch away or to sweep. This may make sense if we think of our sweeping away something at the threshold or opening at our door. When we think of crossing between two realms, we should be able to think of it as those who "cross over" the threshold compared to those who are swept away. When things come to an end, those that don't "cross over" into Yahuah's realm will be swept away.

Zephaniah 1:2 "I will sweep away (**אסף** *asaph) everything from the face of the earth, when I destroy all mankind on the face of the earth," declares Yahuah.*

שפה *sapa* means the edge or to sweep. It also means to establish a border usually by means of fire, as a beacon marking the border, acting as a guiding fire. It is a seashore or a river bank and the edge of the breastplate. It can mean the human lip or in other words language. I find that awe-striking that the word that can mean edge, the threshold, can also mean to sweep, and it can refer to our language.

Genesis 11:1 Now the whole earth had one language and a common speech.

Our words have the power to bring life or death.

Proverbs 15:4 Gentle words bring life and health; a deceitful tongue crushes the Spirit.

If the threshold is a border between two realms, a place that one gets to "cross over" or get swept away, we need to be careful because our words can influence the direction one follows.

אסף *asap* means to gather. That is easy enough to see that it is like gathering ones to "cross over" or gathering ones to be swept away.

יסף *yasap* means to increase. Hopefully we are adding, or increasing, those that will be gathered to cross the threshold.

This final stone, *Yashphey*, seems to reflect those that have crossed over the threshold into the realm of Yahuah's Spiritual place. They are gathered together where they shine, where they are royalty, where they lift up the standard and burn brightly as a beacon, a light on the hill. This stone is that stone of shining brightly, by worshipping Yahuah, gathered at His throne.

Another word that has this **שף** *shaf* or **סף** *saph* phonetic combination is the name Joseph it is spelled **יוסף** *Yoseph*. Do you see the *sp* or *sph* sound again as we saw in our similar roots? Joseph means to increase. Joseph's children are not of Israel; he has Ephraim and Manasseh from an Egyptian wife. They represent those that are grafted in from other people groups. When all comes to an end, at the edge of reeds, some will be swept away and others will cross the threshold. The ones that cross the threshold, whether part of one of the tribes or grafted into one of the tribes, will worship Yahuah. Those that cross over are those that let Yahuah's light shine brightly and are like a beacon defining the edge or the threshold of entering into that inner realm.

Daniel 12:1-3 "At that time Michael, the great prince who protects your people, will arise. There will be a time of distress such as has not happened from the beginning of nations until then. But at that time your people- everyone whose name is found written in the Book- will be delivered. Multitudes who sleep in the dust of the earth will awake; some to everlasting life, others to shame and everlasting contempt. ס *Those who have insight will shine brightly like the brightness of the expanse of heaven and those who lead many to righteousness, like the stars forever.* פ

If you notice I put 2 Hebrew letters in the verse. In Hebrew there is a ס *samekh* between Daniel 12:2 and Daniel 12:3. Then there is a פ *peh* at the end of it. A ס *samekh* is called a *setuma* when used in this form of grammar. It symbols a closed portion. This grammar represents a subdivision in the text. A פ *peh* is called a *petucha* when used in this grammar form. It symbols an open portion. These are grammatical marks but it seems they also represent the lost ones on earth (closed door) and the chosen ones of heaven (open door). I find it interesting that these 2 letters put together are again this *sp* or *sph* combination.

At the end of the row of 12 stones we see this threshold where one is able to shine and cross over to the throne room. Where one can worship and glorify Yahuah with a glowing transparency that truly reflects Him.

This radiating light is apparent even in the physical *Yashphey* stone. The *Yashphey* stone is a translucent gem that glows conspicuously. It attracts attention, it is clearly visible.

Concluding the 12 stones, this last stone of the breastplate shines brightly like a beacon worshipping Yahuah at His throne.

Matthew 5:14-16 You are the light of the world. A town built on a hill cannot be hidden. Neither do people light a lamp and put it under a bowl. Instead they put it on its stand, and it gives light to everyone in the house. In the same way, let your light shine before others, that they may see your good deeds and glorify your Father in heaven.

May we be the brightly shining, fully adorned bride that we are called to be. May we wear His beautiful jewels transparently allowing His light to shine through us and give light to others.

Chapter 26

Applying the Yashphey ישפה *Stone*

1. How do you define worship? How do you worship? Some Hebrew words that can be used for worship include:

לעבד *l'avod*- to work, to serve **להלל** *l'hallel*- to praise **לשיר** *l'shir*- to sing **להודות** *l'hodot*- to give thanks **להתפלל** *l'hitpallel* – to pray

Make a list of some ways you worship Yahuah. Is it in prayer, in singing, in dancing, in serving others? Maybe it is in studying His Word, using your talent, guarding your mouth, obeying His commands.

2. Imagine being in Yahshua's presence. You are His bride walking toward the altar. You have on your shining garments. What things would you say to Him? What things would you thank Him for? What song would you sing to Him? What things would you ask Him about? Would you pray about anything? Pray to Him now, as if He is sitting with you dressed in His beautiful garments, turning His ear to hear your very heart beat.

3. Think of something you need to lift in prayer. Maybe it is something that you have prayed for over a long period of time. Maybe you have a loved one that needs healing, maybe a difficult relationship, maybe a past trauma. As you begin to pray, think of each of the stones and apply each one to your prayer. Example… If I am praying for my marriage, I might apply the stones as follows:

ODEM- Yahshua please help me be still before you as I lift my marriage up to you.

PIT'DAH- Help me be grateful for the gift of marriage you have given me and to be thankful for my spouse.

BAREKET- Line up my thoughts so that Your thoughts of my marriage are like lightning to enter my mind.

NOPHEK- Reach down and scoop this marriage out of the miry clay, set it in the place that you have planned for it.

SAPIR- shape both me and my spouse so that we can be written in Your book.

YAHALAM- hammer out any selfishness in me so that I bring pure oil before you

LESHEM- bring me toward you so that I can wear Your name, and be an example in this marriage

SHEVU- Abba please forgive me for the things I have done that could have hurt my spouse or that have hurt You.

ACHALAMAH- Give me a deep spiritual connection with You. One that stands firm in my correspondence with my spouse.

TARSHISH- let anything that has happened in our marriage be crushed out to the point that there is only joy, help me be a sweet-smelling fragrance.

SHOHAM- Let Your Holy Spirit live in both of us and unite us as one with You.

YASHPHEY- Establish each of us, remind me that I will stand at Your threshold either swept away or crossing over, help me to cross over to You; help me encourage my spouse to cross over the threshold to you also.

4. Go back over each of the stones again and memorize at least one verse for each one. Let that verse be like the glue that helps hold that stone's character in place.

5. Just simply sit in the presence of Yahshua.

CLOSING

Please read. This is more than just ending statements.

I sit in awe of the fact that each one of these precious jewels on the *Choshen Mishpat* have a deep way of showing us what we are to reflect. Each stone is like an opening to get closer to understanding who our Savior is. These stones are transparent. Not only can Yahuah see the depths of who we are, no secrets allowed, no hiding from our sins but also, we reflect Him as we become polished and stop sinning. We must constantly put on our garments of beautiful stones and hear His voice.

Ephesians 6:11-17 Put on all the armor of Yahweh, for you to be able to stand against the strategies of the Devil. For our conflict is not with flesh and blood, but with principalities, and with those in authority, and with the possessors of this dark world, and with the evil spirits that are beneath heaven. Because of this take up all the whole armor of Elohim, that you may be able to resist the evil one, and being prepared you shall prevail. Then stand firm, "having girded your loins about with truth" and having put "on the breastplate of righteousness," and defend your feet with the preparation of the good news of peace. Above all, taking up the shield of faith with which you will be able to quench all the flaming darts of the evil one. Also, put on "the helmet of salvation," and take the sword of the Spirit, which is the word of Yahweh;

There are many other verses in Scripture that mention stones, and I am sure they have a connection in some way. Some of these verses include the following: Genesis 11:1-3: they use brick instead of stone. Genesis 29:1-10: Jacob removes a stone from the well. Joshua 4:2-9: they piled stones as they crossed the Jordan. 1 Kings 5:17-18: Solomon uses stones to build the temple. 1 King 7:9: Solomon used stones in building his house. Ezekiel 36:26: our hearts of stone will be removed. Matthew 24:1-2: Yahshua says the stones will be torn down. Luke 24:1-3: the stone was rolled away. Revelation 2:17: the stone that the builders rejected has become the cornerstone. Exodus 34:1: the Ten Commandments were written on stone. Obviously, there are many rabbit trails we could go down about stones. There is even a description of the King of Tyre wearing the breastplate stones we have studied.

Ezekiel 28:13-15 You have been in Eden, the Garden of Elohim. Every precious stone was your covering; the ruby (Odem), the topaz (Pit'dah), and the diamond (Yahalam), the beryl (Tarshish), the onyx (Shoham), and the jasper (Yashpey), the sapphire (Sapir), the turquoise (Nophek), and the carbuncles (Bareket), and gold; the workmanship of your tambourines and of your pipes in you. In the day you were created they were prepared. You were the cherub that protected with your outstretched wings and I had put you in the holy Mountain of Elohim; where you were. You walked up and down in the midst of the stones of fire. You were perfect in your ways from the day you were created, until iniquity was found in you.

Ezekiel 28:13: lists the stones on the King of Tyre, but there are only nine. Can you list the 3 that are missing? Stop before you keep reading and try to figure it out. The third row of stones

– Leshem, Shevu and Achalamah – are missing. Let's not be like the king of Tyre only emanating a few stones. Let's not pretend to reflect Yahshua but in reality have unrighteousness in us. Instead let's put on the full armor and shine brightly. Let's be what we reflect inside and out.

1st Peter 2:5 You also as living stones are being built into a spiritual house, a holy priesthood, to offer spiritual sacrifices acceptable to Yahweh through Yahshua Messiah.

We are living stones; we are being built; we are putting on our breastplate.

Stones are used to describe strength and resiliency in a person's character. We are living stones being built into a spiritual house. The stones are the foundations. We are spiritual foundations, living stones, with the words of Yahuah written on us. Each stone like each gate has a name of each tribe written on it. It isn't certain which name was on which stone. Maybe we are not able to line up a certain stone with a particular tribe because we are all supposed to be united and need to wear the reflection of the breast plate so that we look like Him. We need to be transparent through and through and let the Spirit shine through us.

Matthew 16:18 I also say to you that you are Peter, and upon this rock I will build My church, and the gates of hell shall not prevail against it.

Revelation 2:17 He who has an ear, let him hear what the Spirit says to the churches. To him who overcomes, to him I will give some of the hidden manna, and I will give him a white stone, and a new name written on the stone which no one knows but he who receives it.

Isaiah 28:16 So Adonai Yahweh says this: Behold, I place in Zion a stone for a foundation, a tried Stone, a precious Cornerstone, a sure Foundation; he who believes shall not hurry.

Matthew 3:9 And do not suppose to say within yourselves, we have a father, Abraham. For I say to you that Yahweh is able to raise up children to Abraham from these stones.

Let's let Him build us up to be the stones that reflect Him.

When Jacob lay his head on a stone, it is actually worded in a way that would make more sense that he lay a stone *by* his head. Some writings suggest that he gathered 12 stones that formed one larger stone. Elijah gathered 12 stones to build an altar. Our breastplate has 12 stones that become one shining light; Yahshuah HaMashiach wears these 12 stones. The stone is Yahshua; the breastplate is Yahshua. May He shine on you so brightly that you reflect Him in all that you do.

I pray that the study of the stones allows you to have a deep understanding of letting Yahuah polish you, raise you up to be a precious stone **אבן** *eben* – one of His children, one of His **בנים** *benim.*

I pray that this study has opened your heart to a desire to reflect our wonderful High Priest, Yahshua, and to wear your stones as a beautiful bride. I pray that every time you think of words used to describe each of the jewels that you have a deep understanding and can be transparent with Yahuah and that you can connect to His transparent love.

Revelation 21:9-27 And one of the seven cherubs came to me, he having the seven bowls being filled with the seven last plagues, and spoke with me, saying, Come, I will show you the bride, the wife of the Lamb. And he carried me in spirit onto a great and high mountain, and showed me the great city, holy Jerusalem, coming down out of Heaven from Yahweh, having the glory of Yahweh. And its light was like a very precious stone, as a jasper (Yashphey) *stone, being clear as crystal, and having a great and high wall, having twelve gates, and twelve cherubs at the gates and names having been inscribed, which the twelve tribes of the sons of Israel. From the east, three gates; from the north, three gates; from the south, three gates; and from the west, three gates. And the wall of the city had twelve foundations, and in them the names of the twelve apostles of the Son. And he speaking with me had a golden reed, that he may measure the city, and its gates and its wall. And the city lies four cornered, even its length as much as the width also. And he measured the city with the reed at twelve thousand furlongs; its length and width and height are equal. And he measured its wall, a hundred and forty four cubits, a measure of a man, which is of a cherub. And the structure of its wall was jasper* (Yashphey)*; and the city was pure gold, like clear glass. The foundation stones of the city wall were adorned with every kind of precious stone. And the foundation of the wall of the city having been adorned with every precious stone: the first foundation, jasper* (Yashphey)*; the second, sapphire* (Sapir)*; the third, chalcedony* (Shevu)*; the fourth, emerald* (Bareket)*; the fifth, sardonyx* (Yahalam)*; the sixth, sardius* (Odem)*; the seventh, chrysolite* (Tarshish)*; the eighth, beryl* (Shoham)*; the ninth, topaz* (Pit'dah)*; the tenth, chrysoprasus* (Nophek)*; the eleventh, hyacinth* (Leshem)*; the twelfth, amethyst* (Achalamah)*. And the twelve gates were twelve pearls; respectively each one of the gates was of one pearl. And the street of the city was pure gold, like transparent glass. And I saw no sanctuary in it, for the Master, Yahweh Almighty, is its sanctuary, and* *the Lamb. And the city had no need of the sun or of the moon, that they might shine in it, for the glory of Yahweh illuminates it, and its lamp is the Lamb. And the nations of the ones saved will walk in its light; and the kings of the earth bring their glory and honor into it. And its gates may not at all be shut by day, for no night will be there. And they will bring the glory and the honor of the nations into it. And there shall not enter it anything that defiles, or he who practices abominations and lies, but only the ones having been written in the Book of Life of the Lamb.*

RESOURCES

Scripture References
Hebraic Roots Bible A Literal Translation. 3rd Edition. Congregation of YHWH, Jerusalem. Word of Truth Publications, 2015.

Hebrew-English Bible. The Bible Society in Israel, 2014.

Chosen Mishpat
Scriptural references as mentioned

https://www.chabad.org/library/article_cdo/aid/3960528/jewish/The-High-Priests-Breastplate-Choshen.htm

Carta's Illustrated Encyclopedia of the Holy Temple in Jerusalem; Israel Ariel Chaim Richman; The Temple Institute Carta, Jerusalem2005 18 Human STREET POB 2500, JERUSALEM 91024, ISRAEL

Ephod
Scriptural references as mentioned

https://www.jewishencyclopedia.com/articles/5790-ephod

Carta's Illustrated Encyclopedia of the Holy Temple in Jerusalem; Israel Ariel Chaim Richman; The Temple Institute Carta, Jerusalem2005 18 Human STREET POB 2500, JERUSALEM 91024, ISRAEL

Hebrew letters
https://www.Ancient-Hebrew.org

https://www.hebrew4christians.com

https://www.chaimbentorah.com

Word studies
https://www.abarim-publications.com

Theological Wordbook of the Old Testament. R. Laird Harris, Gleason L. Archer, Jr., Bruce K. Walk. 1980 The Moody Bible Institute of Chicago , Moody Publishers wordbook

The Brown-Driver-Briggs Hebrew and English Lexicon with and Appendix Containing the Biblical Aramaic. Francis Brown,D.D., D. Litt. Hendrickson Publishing Group. August 2020.

Biographies of those mentioned
Alexander Noble *I Will Die Free.* Noble Alexander with Kay D. Rizzo. Pacific Press Publishing Association, 1998.

Richard Wurmbrand *Tortured for Christ;* Richard Wurmbrand; Westchester, Ill.: Crossway Books, 1987, copyright 1969.

Paul beheaded, Peter crucified upside down, Andrew crucified,Thomas pierced with swords, Phillip arrested and death, Matthew stabbed to death, Bartholomew flayed, James stoned and thrown, Simon killed, Matthais was burned, John boiling oil then Patmos https://overviewbible.com/how-did-the-apostles-die/

Ben stern from Poland
https://www.washingtonpost.com/news/inspired-life/wp/2017/03/02/this-95-year-old-holocaust-survivor-has-a-roommate-shes-a-31-year-old-granddaughter-of-nazis

Folgel Weiss from Czechoslovakia https://www.ushmm.org/remember/holocaust-survivors/volunteers/irene-fogel-weiss

Eva Kor twin Dr Munch Dr Mengele https://people.com/human-interest/holocaust-survivor-eva-kor-dies/Jim Elliot Huron in Ecuador

Jim Elliot *Jim Elliot:One Great Purpose. Christian Heroes: Then &Now.Janet Being and Geoff Being. YWAM Publishing. 1999.*

Elisabeth Elliot https://elisabethelliot.org/about/Mark Twain Strong's Concordance

Other Sources

Urim and Thummim- Egyptian mummies, Babylonian seers Urdu and tamitu, Arabs and 2 rods, Ramses uta, Joseph Smith and the Trim and thummim https://www.jewishencyclopedia.com/articles/14609-urim-and-thummim

Aleph Beta https://www.alephbeta.org/

Mark Twain quote https://www.brainyquote.com/quotes/mark_twain_109919

A. APPENDIX

Letter	Meaning	Contrary Meaning
א	Ox, head, power, strong, leader, oneness, stillness, Elohim, beginning	Theology against Yahuah
ב	Tent, house, heart, floor plan, family, in	Feeling spiritually superior to others
ג	Foot, gather, walk, camel, love, nourishment	Misguided zeal, stepping out of boundary
ד	Door, portal, knowledge, move, entrance	False humility
ה	Man with raised arms, look, reveal, breathe, behold, His feminine nature	Self-deception, self-pity
ו	Tent peg, add, secure, connecting, nail	Anguish, addiction, dependent on something other than Yahuah
ז	Mattock, weapon, cut, nourish	Inappropriate aggression

ח	Tent, wall, outside, divide, half, fence, ladder, prophetic dream	Sin rudeness
ט	Basket, surround, container	Snake
י	arm, closed hand, work, throw, worship, spiritual messenger	No foundation, irrational
כ	Open palm, bend, open, allow, tame, possession, filled with him	Arrogance, seeking one's own will
ל	Shepherd staff, tongue, teach, reaching to heaven, authority, bind	Unwilling to learn, narrow minded, shallow thinking
מ	Water, mighty blood, perfection completion,	Chaos, sorrow, drowning
נ	Seed, fish, continue, heir, son, swimming, prophecy	Thinking you are better than others, aloof
ס	Thorn, support, prop, protect, cover, mysteries of Yahuah	Hate, lack of trust especially toward Yahuah
ע	Eye, see, watch, spiritual discernment, know, shade, rope, trust,	Dark, wicked, covetness

פ	Mouth, open, blow, speaking	Scatter, gossip
צ	Hook, trail, journey, hunt, chase	Self-righteous
ק	Sun on the horizon, condense, circle, time, growth	Monkey, negatively influenced
ר	Head of a man, bending over, willingness, back of head, beginning	Prideful man

Printed in Great Britain
by Amazon

87392113R10119